YORK NOTI

C000045566

York Notes Rapid Revision

Frankenstein

AQA GCSE English Literature

Written by Renée Stanton

Pearson

YORK
PRESS

YORK PRESS
322 Old Brompton Road, London SW5 9JH

PEARSON EDUCATION LIMITED
80 Strand, London, WC2R 0RL

10 9 8 7 6 5 4 3 2 1
ISBN 978–1–2922–7097–5

Phototypeset by Carnegie Book Production
Printed in Slovakia

Photo credits:
IanDagnall Computing/Alamy for page 4 top / IamSuperPear/Shutterstock for page 6
middle / Ellerslie77/© iStock for page 8 bottom / Garrett Aitken/© iStock for page 10
bottom / Dmitry Burlakov/Alamy for page 12 bottom / JRJfin/Shutterstock for page 14
bottom / Sergey Mironov/Shutterstock for page 16 bottom and page 34 top / Oleg
Golovnev/Shutterstock for page 18 bottom / jgroup/© iStock for page 20 bottom /
chirajuti/Shutterstock for page 22 top / Science History Images/Alamy for page 26
middle / Lake Windemere (oil on canvas), Ibbetson, Julius Caesar (1759-1817) / Yale
Center for British Art, Paul Mellon Collection, USA / Bridgeman Images for page 28
middle / retroimages/© iStock for page 30 top / Snopova Elizaveta/Shutterstock for
page 30 bottom / Kozlik/Shutterstock for page 32 top / Kevin McCallum/Alamy for page
36 top / Vasiliy Koval/Shutterstock for page 38 top / Kateryna Yakovlieva/Shutterstock
for page 40 top / Kcirrah/Alamy for page 40 middle / PeopleImages/© iStock for page
42 top / Bannafarsai_Stock/Shutterstock for page 42 bottom / Johan Swanepoel/
Shutterstock for page 46 top / Jacob_09/Shutterstock for page 48 top / Francey/
Shutterstock for page 50 middle / Tinnakorn jorruang/Shutterstock for page 52 bottom /
Andrey_Popov/Shutterstock for page 54 top / Semmick Photo/Shutterstock for page 58
middle / xavierarnau/© iStock for page 60 top

CONTENTS

INTRODUCTION Who was Mary Shelley?

Three key things about Mary Shelley

1. Her parents were William Godwin, the radical philosopher and novelist, and Mary Wollstonecraft, the defender of women's rights.
2. Mary's mother died a few days after giving birth to her.
3. Mary eloped aged sixteen with a married man, Percy Bysshe Shelley. They were later married.

What was her early life like?

- Mary was brought up in London by her father, who remarried. Mary had a difficult relationship with her stepmother.
- Her interest in writing developed early. She was mainly educated at home by tutors, including her father, who strongly influenced her social and political views.
- Her elopement with Percy Bysshe Shelley caused a family uproar. She gave birth to a premature baby who did not survive.

Why did she write *Frankenstein*?

- She wrote a story in the summer of 1816, while on holiday in Switzerland with Shelley and other writers. On a stormy evening they set themselves a ghost story challenge and Mary later developed her story into *Frankenstein*.
- She had been reading several ghost stories but the creative spark for her own story came from a nightmare she'd had of a 'pale student' (Victor) 'kneeling beside the thing he had put together' (from 1831 preface to *Frankenstein*).
- She wanted her story to be as frightening and haunting as her vision.

What was the response to *Frankenstein*?

- The novel was published anonymously and widely reviewed.
- Several reviewers thought it had been written by a man.
- The novel was instantly popular because of its mix of **Gothic** and **realism**.

Letters I–IV

- Walton, an explorer, describes his expedition to the North Pole.
- The crew first glimpse the monster. Then Victor Frankenstein is taken on board.
- Victor promises to tell his story, which Walton records.

Chapters 1–4

- Victor recalls his childhood and how Elizabeth was fostered by his family.
- Victor's scientific interests develop at university.
- Victor obsesses about 'the principle of life' after his mother dies.

Chapters 5–8

- Victor brings the monster to life, rejects him and runs.
- Clerval visits. He realises Victor is ill, stays to nurse him and suggests a walking tour.
- Victor learns of his brother, William's, murder. He realises the monster is the murderer. Justine is accused of William's murder, 'confesses' and is hanged.

Chapters 9–12

- Victor goes to the mountains.
- The monster confronts him and begs him to listen.
- The monster recounts his early experiences and life in the hovel.

Chapters 13–16

- Safie arrives. The reasons for the De Lacey's poverty are explained.
- The monster visits De Lacey. The family flee.
- The monster sets fire to their cottage and leaves for Geneva. When William rejects him, the monster murders William and plants the locket on Justine.

Chapters 17–20

- Victor eventually agrees to the monster's request for a mate.
- Victor reassures his father of his intention to marry Elizabeth, the daughter whom Alphonse had fostered. Victor tours Britain with Clerval before departing alone for the Orkneys.
- Victor creates, then destroys, the female mate. The monster vows revenge. Victor disposes of her body at sea, drifts ashore and is arrested in Ireland for the murder of Clerval.

Chapters 21–24

- Clerval's murder is another of the monster's revenge-killings. Victor is found innocent and set free.
- The monster kills Elizabeth. Alphonse dies of sorrow.
- Victor pursues the monster and dies on Walton's ship. The monster mourns his death.

Three key things about Letters I–IV

1. The progress of **Walton's expedition** is **documented**, alongside the **power, beauty** and **bleakness** of **the Arctic**.
2. The main character, **Victor Frankenstein**, is introduced and a context is provided for his story.
3. Key themes are introduced: **knowledge** and **wisdom, adventure, education, friendship, alienation** and **loneliness**.

What happens in Letters I and II?

- **Letter I:** Walton writes from St Petersburg to reassure his sister, Margaret, of his safety.
- He describes the cold climate and his careful preparations, determination and enthusiasm.
- He outlines his plan to travel to Archangel by sledge and hire a ship and crew.
- **Letter II**: Walton chooses an obedient and courageous crew but feels lonely and in need of a close friend.
- He confesses mixed feelings of pleasure, loneliness and fear when he considers the possible dangers lying ahead.

What happens in Letters III and IV?

- **Letter III**: Having embarked on his journey, Walton feels a great responsibility to his ship and crew but also a desire to take risks in order to pursue his goal to reach the North Pole.
- **Letter IV**: The ice-bound crew catch sight of a **'gigantic'** man on a sledge in the distance, heading northwards.
- After the thaw, the crew see another man, adrift on the ice but close to the ship, who is welcomed on board.
- Walton warms towards this man, who has been in pursuit of somebody and is physically and emotionally exhausted.
- Walton confides in him about his ambitions but the man responds with despair, promising to tell a story of his own as a warning to Walton.

Five key quotations

1. Walton on discovery and exploration: 'I shall satiate my ardent curiosity with the sight of a part of the world never before visited' (Letter I)

2. Walton on friendship: 'I desire the company of a man who could sympathise with me; whose eyes would reply to mine.' (Letter II)

3. Walton's desire for glory: 'But success *shall* crown my endeavours.' (Letter III)

4. First description of the monster – Walton: 'a being which had the shape of man, but apparently of gigantic stature' (Letter IV)

5. Victor's warning to Walton: 'You seek for knowledge and wisdom … I ardently hope that the gratification of your wishes may not be a serpent to sting you, as mine has been.' (Letter IV)

Note it!

These four letters provide an opening frame to the novel, in epistolary form. The novel, however, does not continue to be written in letters and Walton, the letter writer, is not the main character of the novel as might have been expected.

Exam focus

How can I write about Walton's opening letters? AO2

You can use these letters to write about Walton's mindset as an explorer.

Walton's opening letters reveal someone obsessed by exploration. He writes grandly: 'I shall satiate my ardent curiosity with the sight of a part of the world never before visited'. He uses powerfully emotional language, such as the verb 'satiate', the adjective 'ardent' and the phrase 'never before' to convey his desire to be the first to make his mark on the North Pole. His passion for adventure, discovery and glory mirrors that of Victor.	Topic sentence refers to Walton's letters
	Relevant quotation is fluently embedded
	Explains quotation and comments on language
	Makes a structural link with Victor's character

Now you try!

Finish this paragraph about Walton's letters. Use one of the quotations from the list.

Walton's letters introduce the important theme of friendship when ....

Five key things about Chapters 1-4

1. **Victor's parents** provide him with **stability**, a **happy childhood** and a set of **moral values**, ideas revisited in Victor's relationship with the monster.

2. Victor is attached to his **foster sister, Elizabeth,** and his **friend, Clerval.** Both are **very different from Victor** but are **much-loved companions.**

3. **Themes** of **science** and **knowledge** are introduced and **Victor's** early **unchecked interest in the world's 'secrets'** develops at university into a **desire to create life.**

4. Victor's **deteriorating health** and **behaviour foreshadow** a **more serious decline.**

5. Linked themes are introduced: **family, love, kindness** and **friendship.**

What happens in Chapters 1 and 2?

- Alphonse, Victor's father, is a 'syndic' or magistrate. Late in life he marries Caroline, the poor, orphaned daughter of his deceased best friend.

- They are happily married and have a family of their own as well as fostering an orphan, Elizabeth.

- Victor's passion for life's mysteries contrasts with Elizabeth's appreciation of poetry and nature and Clerval's interest in chivalry and romance.

- Alphonse's disregard for the writer Cornelius Agrippa encourages, rather than deters, Victor's reading. This develops into an obsession with immortality, eternal youth and raising ghosts and devils.

- A lightning strike develops Victor's interest in galvanism – the use of electric currents to create movement in the muscles of animal corpses.

What happens in Chapters 3 and 4?

- Caroline dies, having sacrificed her own health to nurse Elizabeth. Her death-bed wish is that Victor and Elizabeth marry.

- Victor departs for university alone, without Clerval, whose merchant father does not value an extended education. There Victor focuses on creating life from the dead, to the detriment of his health and family relationships.

Five key quotations

1. Clerval's goodness: 'could aught ill entrench on the noble spirit of Clerval?' (Chapter 2)
2. Elizabeth's goodness: 'The saintly soul of Elizabeth shone like a shrine-dedicated lamp' (Chapter 2)
3. Victor's use of **hyperbole** about his childhood: 'No human being could have passed a happier childhood' (Chapter 2)
4. Victor's thirst for learning: 'It was the secrets of heaven and earth that I desired to learn' (Chapter 2)
5. Waldman to Victor on the achievements of modern scientists: '"They penetrate into the recesses of nature, and show how she works in her hiding places."' (Chapter 3)

Note it!

There are hints that Victor feels his father could have better guided his reading or explained why a writer such as Agrippa was **'sad trash'**. Victor also suggests that his father might be partly to blame for his **'ruin'**.

Exam focus

How can I write about Victor's childhood? AO1

You can explore the joy of Victor's childhood depicted in Chapters 1–4.

Victor's childhood is presented as idyllic. He categorically states: 'No human being could have passed a happier childhood'. He sees himself as the most fortunate child, using hyperbole for emphasis in the phrase 'No human being' and reinforcing this idea with the intensifying phrase 'happier'. He is nostalgic as he looks back from a position of ruin and misery.	Topic sentence refers to Victor's childhood
	Quotation is fluently embedded
	Explains quotation and comments on language
	Develops a linking and explanatory point

Now you try!

Finish this paragraph about the function of the first four chapters. Use one of the quotations from the list.

The first four chapters introduce Victor's childhood interests and in particular his thirst for learning, when ....

Five key things about Chapters 5-8

1. Victor **succeeds in creating** the monster but **misunderstands** and **rejects** it.
2. **Clerval's devotion** represents ideals of **love**, **responsibility** and **friendship**.
3. In letters, Elizabeth tells Victor of the **return of Justine Moritz**, a much-loved **servant** of **the Frankensteins**, and his father tells him of **William's murder**.
4. The **monster's brief appearance** to Victor **in the mountains** makes Victor realise that the **monster is William's murderer**.
5. **Justine's wrongful execution** and **William's death** emphasise the **tragic repercussions** of Victor's actions.

What happens in Chapters 5 and 6?

- The monster is brought to life in Victor's workshop and Victor's initial reaction of 'horror and disgust' foreshadows much of what is to come.
- In a nightmare Victor kisses Elizabeth, who turns into his dead mother. He wakes up to find the monster at his bedside, and flees, despite its signs of friendship.
- Clerval comes to visit Victor the next morning, stays, nurses him and proposes walking therapy, which temporarily lifts Victor's spirits.
- A letter from Elizabeth brings news of Justine's return to the Frankensteins, after her mother's death.

What happens in Chapters 7 and 8?

- A letter from Alphonse brings news of William's murder.
- On his way home, Victor sees the monster in the mountains, just after addressing William's spirit. He connects the monster with William's murder.
- Justine is arrested and put on trial for William's murder. She is incriminated by having the locket which Elizabeth had let William wear.
- After being bullied into confessing, Justine is hanged. Elizabeth's speech in Justine's defence is disregarded.
- Victor agonises over his guilt in causing so much grief to his family.

Five key quotations

1. The monster comes to life: 'I saw the dull yellow eye of the creature open' (Chapter 5)

2. The monster's first communication attempt: 'His jaws opened, and he muttered some inarticulate sounds, while a grin wrinkled his cheeks.' (Chapter 5)

3. Clerval's positive influence: 'Clerval called forth the better feelings of my heart' (Chapter 6)

4. Elizabeth to Justine on female goodness: 'I will melt the stony hearts of your enemies by my tears and prayers.' (Chapter 8)

5. Victor's guilt: 'William and Justine, the first hapless victims to my unhallowed arts' (Chapter 8)

Note it!

Victor's belief that nobody else's suffering is as bad as his can be seen as self-centred. Justine is **'sustained by innocence'** whereas **'fangs of remorse'** tear him. The language of his pain is more violent than the imagined pain of others. His use of abstract nouns and Faustian imagery adds emphasis.

Exam focus

How can I write about Victor's response to the monster? AO1

You can refer to Victor's negative response to the monster's first actions.

Victor's initial response to the monster is fear and incomprehension.	Topic sentence refers to Victor's response
He describes how its 'jaws opened, and he muttered some inarticulate sounds, while a grin wrinkled his cheeks'.	Quotation is fluently embedded
Victor sees his creation in terms of body parts such as 'jaws' and 'cheeks' and is blind to the possibility that the 'grin' and 'inarticulate sounds' are attempts at friendship.	Explains quotation and comments on language
From the outset Victor perceives the monster negatively and this persists throughout much of the novel.	Develops the point

Now you try!

Finish this paragraph about Chapters 5–8. Use one of the quotations from the list.

The important theme of female goodness is explored in Chapter 8 when Elizabeth ....

PLOT AND STRUCTURE Chapters 9-12

Five key things about Chapters 9-12

1. **Men and monsters** are **frequently compared**, notably by **Elizabeth's** statement **'men appear to me as monsters'** and also by **Victor's** observations and behaviour.
2. The **monster speaks to Victor** for the **first time**.
3. The monster's story begins in **Chapter 11**, where the **narrative voice changes from Victor's to the monster's**. There is a contrast between the **monster's archaic language** learned from books and **Victor's educated**, but more **natural-sounding, language**.
4. The **monster's** experience of **abandonment** is the **antithesis** of Victor's comfortable childhood.
5. The **De Laceys** provide a **positive model** of **family relationships**.

What happens in Chapters 9 and 10?

- Victor escapes from his misery over William's death to the isolation and comfort of the natural world in Chamonix.
- The awe-inspiring view at the top of Montanvert makes Victor speak aloud. The monster instantly appears.
- The monster understands Victor's hostility but questions his sense of duty and appeals to his better nature.
- The monster demands the right to tell his story and gives Victor the choice of acting kindly towards him or being the **'author'** of his own **'ruin'**.

What happens in Chapters 11 and 12?

- The monster recollects his experiences in the natural world and his first interactions with humans.
- In a **'hovel'** next to the De Laceys, the monster observes their behaviour, emotions and routines as well as admiring their **'gentle manners'**.
- The monster secretly helps them, gradually masters language and, despite the shock of seeing his own reflection, remains happy and hopeful.

Five key quotations

1. Men and monsters – Victor about himself: 'the fiend that lurked in my heart' (Chapter 9)
2. Victor on the healing qualities of nature: 'The very winds whispered in soothing accents' (Chapter 9)
3. The monster negotiates his terms with Victor: 'I am thy creature, and I will be even mild and docile to my natural lord and king, if thou wilt also perform thy part' (Chapter 10)
4. The monster's curiosity about the De Laceys: 'I longed to discover the motives and feelings of these lovely creatures.' (Chapter 12)
5. The monster's excitement at mastering language: 'I cannot describe the delight I felt when I learned the ideas appropriated to each of these sounds' (Chapter 12)

Note it!

When in mourning for William and Justine, Elizabeth's language suggests an uncanny understanding of what has happened: **'men appear to me as monsters thirsting for each other's blood'.** She is unsettled by the **'expression of despair, and … revenge'** on Victor's face.

Exam focus

How can I write about the monster's voice?

You can analyse the monster's tone in dialogue and monologue.

> The monster's voice is heard in conversation with Victor. His ability to negotiate is shown in the formal archaic language: 'I am thy creature, and I will be even mild and docile to my natural lord and king, if thou wilt also perform thy part'. His subservience is signalled by 'thy creature' but his terms are outlined in the conditions of the 'if' clause. His speech style reveals respect for Victor and a desire to be respected.

| Topic sentence refers to monster's voice |
| Quotation is fluently embedded |
| Explains quotation and comments on language |
| Develops and summarises point |

Now you try!

Finish this paragraph about the theme of human understanding. Use one of the quotations from the list.

The monster's natural curiosity about humans is explored in Chapter 12 when..........

PLOT AND STRUCTURE Chapters 13-16

Five key things about Chapters 13-16

1. The **De Laceys' sad history** and link to **Safie** is a **story within a story**. Its themes of injustice, exclusion and betrayal **mirror the main story**.
2. The effect of **reading** on the monster's knowledge and understanding of the world links with Victor's passion for **book learning**.
3. The monster's visit to De Lacey leads to a **tragic sequence of events**, resulting in **chaos**, **rejection**, **injustice** and **murder**.
4. The **themes** of **kindness** and **respect** are developed in the presentation of the De Laceys.
5. The **themes** of **learning** and **knowledge** are explored through the monster's education.

What happens in Chapters 13 and 14?

- Safie arrives at the De Laceys. The monster observes how her appearance and language differ from the others and her positive effect on the family and Felix in particular.
- He listens and learns about human nature when Felix teaches Safie to read.
- He learns about the De Laceys' history, the reason for their poverty and their connection with Safie.

What happens in Chapters 15 and 16?

- The three books the monster reads independently make him think deeply. He also reads Victor's journal, which saddens him.
- He visits De Lacey and tells him of his desire to **'claim the protection of some friends'**. De Lacey treats him with respect.
- The family arrive home to find the monster and are horrified. They flee. Hurt and enraged, the monster sets fire to their cottage and leaves to find Victor.
- The monster's motivation in rescuing the drowning girl is misunderstood. In seeking out an unprejudiced child, he ends up murdering William and planting incriminating evidence on Justine. His alienation makes him want a female companion **'of the same species'** with **'the same defects'**.

Five key quotations

1. The monster to Victor on knowledge: 'Of what a strange nature is knowledge! It clings to the mind ... like a lichen on the rock.' (Chapter 13)

2. His developing sense of a negative identity: 'but my form is a filthy type of yours' (Chapter 15)

3. The monster identifies with Satan: 'I, like the arch-fiend, bore a hell within me' (Chapter 16)

4. His anger against Victor: 'Unfeeling, heartless creator!' (Chapter 16)

5. The monster's alienation: 'I am alone, and miserable; man will not associate with me' (Chapter 16)

Note it!

Books transform the monster's thinking and imagination. *Ruins of Empires* informs him about history. Adam and Satan are characters he can identify with in *Paradise Lost*. Plutarch's *Lives* heightens his understanding of morality. *The Sorrows of Werther* provokes empathy. They all have a humanising effect.

Exam focus

How can I write about the monster's feeling of alienation? AO1

You can explore the monster's increasing feelings of alienation in his **dialogue** with De Lacey.

The monster gradually loses hope of being accepted by humans. The poignant statement 'I am alone, and miserable; man will not associate with me' expresses understanding of the cause of his misery and a certainty that it is permanent. The use of the verb 'will' expresses this certainty as well as a feeling of resignation. His realisation paves the way for the request for a mate who will accept him.

Topic sentence refers to alienation

Quotation is fluently embedded

Explains quotation and comments on language

Moves on the argument

Now you try!

Finish this paragraph about theme linking to structure. Use one of the quotations from the list.

The significant theme of knowledge is developed in Chapter 13 when.................................

Five key things about Chapters 17–20

1. **Victor** takes over the narrative and **recounts** an extended **discussion with the monster**.
2. The **monster's desire** for a **mate** parallels **Victor's desire to marry**.
3. Victor's narrative digression gives Walton (and the reader) **foreknowledge of Clerval's death**, long before he describes its actual circumstances.
4. Two narrative elements are motifs; **Victor's creative isolation** and **the monster's** appearance with a **'grin'**.
5. **Victor's destruction** of the **female mate**, in full view of the monster, is an important **narrative turning point**. The monster's threats foreshadow future narrative events.

What happens in Chapters 17 and 18?

- Victor is with the monster in the mountains.
- The monster commands Victor to make him a mate. Victor initially refuses. He eventually agrees, but only if the monster and his mate go into exile.
- Victor reassures Alphonse of his intention to marry Elizabeth. He needs to create the monster's female mate first, so asks for some time to visit England, keeping the reason for his journey secret. Clerval accompanies Victor.

What happens in Chapters 19 and 20?

- Victor and Clerval arrive in Britain. The anxious Victor suggests they part company in Scotland and he travels alone to the isolated Orkneys.
- Victor imagines the mate refusing to agree to exile or the monsters' offspring breeding **'a race of devils'** that curse the earth.

- The monster appears and Victor, sensing **'malice and treachery'**, brutally destroys his mate. The monster leaves in anguish.
- The monster returns and, after making a series of threats, escapes before Victor can seize him.
- Victor gets rid of his tools and the body at sea, drifts off course and is arrested in Ireland for the murder of Clerval.

Five key quotations

1. The monster's persuasive power: 'If I have no ties and no affections, hatred and vice must be my portion' (Chapter 17)
2. Clerval as protector: 'Henry might stand between me and the intrusion of my foe.' (Chapter 18)
3. Victor's spiritual death: 'But I am a blasted tree; the bolt has entered my soul' (Chapter 19)
4. The monster's final threat: 'I shall be with you on your wedding-night.' (Chapter 20)
5. After destroying the mate, Victor feels almost as if he had: 'mangled the living flesh of a human being' (Chapter 20)

Note it!

Victor worries that the female mate might have opinions and thoughts conflicting with the monster's; murderous and **'more malignant'** intentions; feelings of sexual disgust and hatred, and a reproductive capacity that could become a curse to humans.

Exam focus

How can I write about the monster's power?

You can write about the monster's skills of persuasion over Victor.

> Shelley shows the monster's power when persuading Victor to make him a mate. His reasoning: 'If I have no ties and no affections, hatred and vice must be my portion' reveals an understanding that lack of love and friendship lead to alienation and immorality. The repetition of 'no' emphasises the negativity of this state of mind and 'must' expresses its inevitability. It is the monster's rhetorical power that moves Victor here.

Topic sentence refers to monster's power

Quotation is fluently embedded

Explains quotation and comments on language

Point on power is summarised

Now you try!

Finish this paragraph about structure. Use one of the quotations from the list.

After the destruction of his mate, the monster's final threat foreshadows Elizabeth's death with..

PLOT AND STRUCTURE Chapters 21–24

Five key things about Chapters 21-24

1. The **discovery** of the **murder victim's identity** (Clerval) heightens the dramatic tension.

2. **Victor's** arrest, imprisonment and trial **parallel** that of **Justine's.**

3. **Tension rises** with the approach of Victor and Elizabeth's wedding and the **narrative** foreshadowing of tragedy.

4. **Victor's** hunt for the monster generates the **final piece of narrative action**, which takes the reader and Walton to the **narrative present** on the ship.

5. **Paired** themes are developed: justice and freedom; dream/nightmare and reality; life and death.

What happens in Chapters 21 and 22?

● Victor is with a magistrate and hears the statements of those who either witnessed seeing a man in a boat or discovered the corpse.

● Victor collapses when he realises that the corpse is Clerval, overcome by horror and guilt. He is subsequently imprisoned for Clerval's murder.

● Alphonse visits Victor, who is set free once his innocence is proved. They travel back home via Paris, where Victor receives a letter from Elizabeth, declaring her love but expressing concern that Victor might love another.

● Victor writes to reassure her, also informing her of a secret he has to reveal once they are married.

● Victor returns home, expresses his guilt, tries to bury his anxiety and puts his energies into protecting his family. Victor and Elizabeth marry.

What happens in Chapters 23 and 24?

● The monster murders Elizabeth on their wedding night. Alphonse dies of grief.

● Victor tells a local magistrate about the monster. The man is sympathetic but pragmatic and Victor decides he must act alone, outside the law.

● Victor visits the family graves, calls to the spirits, hears the monster laughing and pursues him to the Arctic. He is rescued by Walton's crew and asks Walton to kill the monster on his behalf.

Five key quotations

1. Victor on the blurring of dream and reality: 'The whole series of my life appeared to me as a dream' (Chapter 21)
2. Victor's guilt: 'William, Justine, and Henry – they all died by my hands.' (Chapter 22)
3. Victor's loss of hope: 'but the apple was already eaten' (Chapter 22)
4. Nightmarish imagery of Elizabeth: 'her bloodless arms and relaxed form flung by the murderer on its bridal bier' (Chapter 23)
5. Victor addresses the spirits: 'Let the cursed and hellish monster drink deep of agony' (Chapter 24)

Note it!

Elizabeth is murdered on the night of her wedding. The union is never consummated and the marital bed becomes a **'bier'**, a frame to support a corpse or coffin. Victor's decision to go back on his promise to create a female mate results in a calculated payback.

Exam focus

How can I write about Victor's guilt?

You can write about how Victor's guilt is expressed in these chapters.

> Victor's guilt becomes more intense as the narrative tension rises. His statement 'William, Justine and Henry - they all died by my hands' expresses a deep sense of guilt even if not literally true. The word 'all' is emphatic and the phrase 'by my hands' provides an image of the means of death, by strangling, as well as a more abstract meaning of responsibility. Victor's confession is metaphorically true as he believes he is guilty.

Topic sentence refers to Victor's guilt

Quotation is fluently embedded

Explains quotation and comments on language

Summarises point

Now you try!

Finish this paragraph about structure. Use one of the quotations from the list.

It is at this point in the narrative that Shelley shows Victor's loss of hope of leading a meaningful life, when ....

PLOT AND STRUCTURE Walton, in continuation

Five key things about Walton's continuation in letters

1. **Walton** continues the narrative in epistolary form. The reader realises **his role** in the **preservation and construction of Victor's narrative**.

2. Walton insists on the **truth of Victor's narrative**, alluding to the **evidence** of Felix and Safie's **letters** and his **sighting of the monster**.

3. **Victor participates** in some **narrative action**. The **crew question Walton's judgement** and **Victor supports him**. **Walton's agreement** to the crew's request **echoes Victor's agreement** to the monster's request for a mate.

4. The story reaches its climax when **Walton enters Victor's cabin**, to find the **grief-stricken monster** at the dead Victor's side. The monster **challenges the narrative** bias in Victor's story by telling of his own agonies.

5. The **narrative action ends** with the **monster's plan** to take his life.

What happens in Letters 1 and 2?

- On board ship, Walton gets to know Victor and listens to and records his story in his letters.

- Walton admires Victor, desiring his friendship, but Victor's mind is fixed on death, that of the monster and his own.

- Walton describes the dangers, his duty to the crew and his fears of mutiny.

What happens in Letters 3-5?

- The crew ask Walton to abort the expedition. Victor intervenes, trying to dissuade them.

- Walton reluctantly agrees to the crew's request. The ice cracks and the crew's delight wakes Victor. Walton hears Victor's last words.

- Later, Walton returns to Victor's cabin to find the monster, distressed, at Victor's bedside. Walton wants to destroy the monster on Victor's behalf but **'curiosity and compassion'** prevent him.

- The monster gives his version of events and reveals his wish to take his life. He leaves the cabin via the window, takes his 'ice-raft' and is soon **'lost in darkness and distance'**.

Five key quotations

1. Victor's youthful ambition: 'I trod heaven in my thoughts' (Letter 1)
2. Walton's sense of responsibility: 'If we are lost, my mad schemes are the cause.' (Letter 2)
3. Victor's appeal to the crew: 'Oh! be men, or be more than men.' (Letter 3)
4. The monster's lament: 'what does it avail that I now ask thee to pardon me?' (Letter 5)
5. The monster's plan for his suicide: 'I shall collect my funeral pile and consume to ashes this miserable frame' (Letter 5)

Note it!

Shelley draws a parallel between Victor and the monster when both refer to death as an escape from life's agonies. Victor refers to it as **'happy'**, seeing the forms of his **'beloved dead'** and wanting to **'hasten to their arms'** (p.166). The monster refers to it as his **'only consolation'** (p. 170).

Exam focus

How can I write about the monster's intention to take his own life? AO1

You can explore the monster's agony and wish for death once he knows Victor has died.

The monster's desire to take his own life expresses his desire for autonomy. Shelley uses active language for this purpose: 'I shall collect my funeral pile and consume to ashes this miserable frame'. The pronoun 'I' expresses his agency – he is the one who is collecting and consuming. The phrase 'this miserable frame' suggests how his body identifies him in a negative way, almost as if it does not belong to him.

Topic sentence refers to his death wish	
Quotation is fluently embedded	
Explains and comments on language	
Develops another comment on language	

Now you try!

Finish this paragraph about parallels between characters. Use one of the quotations from the list.

In the final letters, Shelley contrasts Victor and Walton when she demonstrates Walton's sense of responsibility...

Three key things about form and structure

1. The novel is a **mix of** genres: the Gothic, science fiction and cautionary tale.

2. Three first-person narrators produce three different versions of the story.

3. The **novel's core** is the **monster's story, framed by Victor's story**, in turn **framed by Walton's story.** This framed narration structure is like a set of objects fitting inside each other, sometimes called a 'Chinese box' or 'Russian doll' structure.

How does Shelley use time in *Frankenstein*?

- The novel is non-chronological because events are not presented in time order. It begins near the end of the plot when Walton's crew see the monster and meet Victor.

- Victor's narration, starting with his past, continues chronologically until the monster appears, demanding that Victor listen to his story.

- The monster begins with an extended flashback and ends by demanding a mate. Victor then resumes his story until his death requires Walton's 'continuation'.

How does Shelley use stories within stories?

- Walton's framing letters generate feelings of uncertainty, danger and realism – a sense of Walton recording events that catch up with him.

- His story of Arctic discovery is displaced by the recording of Victor's life.

- Walton tells Victor's story who, in turn, tells the monster's story. Victor's references to Walton remind the reader of his presence.

How does Shelley use narrative patterns?

- Recurring themes generate narrative patterns. Journeys take place in the real world and in the narrators' minds.

- Walton's letters emphasise absence from home and family. Victor's home and family are all important. The monster yearns for both.

- Foreshadowing creates tension, e.g. when the monster states he will be there on Victor's wedding night and when Victor hints at Clerval's death.

Five key quotations

1. Victor's story to Walton begins: 'I am by birth a Genevese; and my family is one of the most distinguished of that republic.' (Chapter 1)
2. The monster's story to Victor begins: 'It is with considerable difficulty that I remember the original era of my being' (Chapter 11)
3. The monster's story to Victor ends: 'and fear not but that when you are ready I shall appear' (Chapter 17)
4. Victor's story to Walton ends: 'thrust your sword into his heart. I will hover near and direct the steel aright.' (Chapter 24)
5. Walton's final words about the monster: 'He was soon borne away by the waves and lost in darkness and distance.' (Letter 5)

Note it!

The way Shelley mixes genres reflects diverse cultural interests. She explores developments in science and global discovery, as well as Gothic moments of misery and horror. The cautionary tale element derives from the dangers of Victor's limitless pursuit of knowledge.

Exam focus

How can I write about stories within stories?

You can write about the three narratives that sit within each other.

The novel is a series of stories within stories, known as framed narration. The monster's story, embedded in Victor's story, itself framed by Walton's story, begins quietly: 'It is with considerable difficulty that I remember the original era of my being'. The language is formal and the tone honest as the monster recollects. Its touching quality contrasts with Victor's proud reference to his birthright as he begins his story.	Introduces point about form
	Relevant evidence with embedded quotation
	Analyses use of language and style
	Develops point, with effect on reader

Now you try!

Finish this paragraph about form. Use one of the quotations from the list.

Foreshadowing is an aspect of narrative form used throughout to raise dramatic tension; for example, in the monster's warning ....

1. Look at this ideas map representing Walton's letters I–IV.
   Is there anything else you could add?

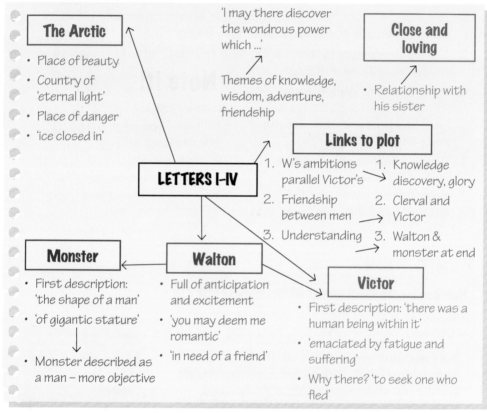

2. Create your own ideas map for one of the other chapters.

Quick quiz

Answer these quick questions about plot and structure.

1. Why does Victor decide to tell Walton his story?
2. How does Alphonse meet his wife, Caroline?
3. How does Elizabeth become part of Victor's family?
4. What was the occupation of Clerval's father and why is it important to the plot?
5. What was Alphonse's occupation?

6. Which writer does Alphonse disapprove of Victor reading?
7. How does Caroline die?
8. Who arrives the morning after the monster's 'birth'?
9. What happens when Victor addresses the dead spirit of William on his way home?
10. Why does Elizabeth initially blame herself for William's death?
11. Why is Justine accused of William's murder and why does she 'confess'?
12. Why does Victor go to Chamonix?
13. What happens at the top of the Montanvert mountain?
14. Who is in love with Safie?
15. What does the monster discover about the De Laceys' connection with Safie?
16. Why does the monster decide to visit old De Lacey?
17 What does the monster specify about the female mate and why?
18 Why does Victor suddenly destroy the female mate?
19. What are the monster's last words to Victor in Orkney?
20. What does the monster intend to do at the end of the novel?

Power paragraphs

Write **a paragraph** in response to **each of these questions**. For each, try to **use one quotation** you have learned from this section.

1. How does Shelley describe the Arctic in the first four letters?
2. What impression do you have of the relationship between Walton and his sister, Margaret, from the first four letters?

Exam practice

Re-read the section in Letter II from 'But I have one want which I have never yet been able to satisfy' to 'endeavour to regulate my mind'.

What does this extract tell the reader about how Walton sees himself?

Write **two paragraphs** explaining your ideas. You could write about:

- Walton's education and character
- Walton's desire for a close friend.

Five key things about science and revolution

1. Shelley was writing in an **age of scientific discovery**. The British scientist **Humphrey Davy** believed in **science's potential** to shape the future and give mankind **'creative' powers over nature**.

2. Another area of scientific interest was in **galvanism** – **'animating' animal corpses** through an **electrical charge**.

3. It was a time of **political and social instability. Industrialisation** was changing people's lives, sometimes for the worse.

4. The **Luddite Riots** (1811–16) involved the **destruction of labour-saving textile machinery** by **workers** who **feared losing their jobs** and their skills. Some were **executed**. The **middle-classes feared 'mob violence'**, where workers turned against their masters.

5. The **effects of the French Revolution** (1789) were **far-reaching**, and ideas of power and the rules of society were being challenged **across Europe**.

How is science reflected in *Frankenstein?*

- Shelley went to one of Davy's lectures with her father in 1812. Davy's ideas of man's creativity and mastery of nature are reflected in Victor.

- Shelley was familiar with Galvani's and Aldini's electrical experimentation. Victor's animation of the monster is reminiscent of their work.

- Shelley describes different states of being, e.g. life, death and some in-between states such as fainting, coma and sleeping. These descriptions reflect scientific interest of the time in the states that were named 'apparent death', 'absolute death' and 'suspended animation'.

How is revolution reflected in *Frankenstein?*

- The monster's rage may reflect the political instability at home and abroad, e.g. the monster is symbolic of the threat of 'mob violence'. His wish and need to be listened to and respected can be seen as representing the revolutionary element of society.

- Victor's desire to create can be seen as a revolutionary act as it challenges established conventions and beliefs.

What was the scientific interest in the states of life and death?

- Interest grew in resuscitation – bringing back to life those appearing to be dead. In 1744 the 'Society for the Recovery of Persons Apparently Drowned' was set up. Shelley's mother was revived after jumping off Putney Bridge.

- Shelley uses this scientific language to describe her characters' crises, e.g. after animating the monster, Victor is **'lifeless'**; Clerval **'restored'** him to **'life'**.

Three key quotations

1. Victor animates the monster: 'I collected the instruments of life ... that I might infuse a spark of being into the lifeless thing' (Chapter 5)

2. Victor, holding Elizabeth's corpse: 'but the deadly langour and coldness of the limbs ... had ceased to be the Elizabeth whom I had loved and cherished' (Chapter 23)

3. The monster's threat: 'Yet mine shall not be the submission of abject slavery. I will revenge my injuries' (Chapter 17)

Note it!

Shelley's father, William Godwin, believed in the individual's rational sense to develop moral and political understanding. He was also concerned about abuses of power. The monster's character and situation reflect these ideas.

Exam focus

How do I link context to the novel?

You can explain why Shelley uses scientific methods of the time.

Victor's experimentation reflects Shelley's knowledge of Galvini's work on 'animal electricity'. The monster's	Topic sentence
'convulsive motion' and 'dull yellow eye' echoes his real-life descriptions. Galvini worked with dismembered	Relevant quotation embedded
animals, whose legs were seen to twitch or eyes open. Aldini later used a convict's corpse. Similarly, Victor's	Point on context developed
science is presented as both secretive and immoral.	Links context to theme

Now you try!

Finish this paragraph on social unrest. Use one of the quotations from the list.

Shelley explores the context of revolution when the monster threatens Victor with ....

Five key things about Romanticism and the Gothic

1. **Romanticism** in literature and art focussed on ideas of the imagination; the power and beauty of nature; and freedom and innocence in childhood.

2. *Frankenstein* is considered a Romantic novel because it deals with **themes** associated with Romanticism – not 'romantic' in the modern sense.

3. The **Gothic** novel often features the **uncanny**; abuse of power; violence against women; intense feelings; dreams and nightmares; gloomy, isolated settings; themes of revenge; and breaking the rules of nature.

4. Gothic novels often contain mystery, a hunt/chase or horror elements. These are all present in *Frankenstein.*

5. Romanticism and the Gothic are useful terms to describe *Frankenstein* but the novel is hard to categorise because of its originality.

How does Shelley use Romanticism in *Frankenstein?*

- Victor, Walton and Clerval can be seen as Romantic characters, full of passion, dreams and idealism.
- The beauty of the natural world figures highly. Clerval celebrates nature's healing qualities. There are several descriptions of **sublime** landscapes and use of **pathetic fallacy.**
- The monster's early experiences have a Romantic, childlike quality.
- Spiritual thoughts and intense feelings recur, such as awe and fascination.

How does Shelley use the Gothic in *Frankenstein?*

- Victor is full of fear, misery, terror and guilt – intense and excessive feelings.
- The monster haunts Victor, committing brutal acts in order to have revenge.
- Victor breaks both moral rules and the laws of nature, e.g. by taking corpses from graves.
- His obsession leads him to isolated places: his workshop **'of filthy creation'**, prison, the Orkneys, the Arctic.
- Women are placed in danger and suffer violence at the hands of men.

How are Romanticism and the Gothic personally linked to Shelley?

- Mary Shelley was with several Romantic writers, including her lover, Percy Bysshe Shelley, at the Villa Diodati, when she started writing *Frankenstein*. It was her response to their ghost story writing challenge.
- In her preface to *Frankenstein* she aims: **'to curdle the blood and quicken the beatings of the heart'**. Horror and terror is linked with the Gothic.

Three key quotations

1. Romanticism in Victor: 'Clerval called forth the better feelings of my heart; he again taught me to love the aspect of nature, and the cheerful faces of children.' (Chapter 6)

2. The Gothic in Victor: 'Who shall conceive the horrors of my secret toil, as I dabbled among the unhallowed damps of the grave ...?' (Chapter 4)

3. Romanticism mixed with Gothic – in Victor: 'From my infancy I was imbued with high hopes and a lofty ambition ... you would not recognise me in this state of degradation.' (Walton, in continuation)

Note it!

The Gothic can be seen as a type of Romanticism where dreams become nightmares, power is used for evil and innocence is degraded by experience.

Exam focus

How do I link context to the novel?

You can show how context adds depth to a theme.

	Topic sentence
Shelley was living when graveyard bodysnatching was a	Point on context introduced
lucrative business. Doctors needed bodies to practise dissection and paid bodysnatchers to dig up freshly	Relevant quotation embedded
buried corpses. Victor is bodysnatching in the Gothic 'unhallowed damps of the grave' at his 'secret toil'.	Context linked to the Gothic

Now you try!

Finish this paragraph about the novel's context. Use one of the quotations from the list.

Shelley presents Clerval as a Romantic figure when..

SETTING AND CONTEXT Settings

Five key things about settings in the novel

1. Most exterior settings in *Frankenstein* are huge, remote landscapes where the monster ranges freely, e.g. the Arctic, the Alps and, on a smaller scale, the Orkneys.

2. Most interior settings are gloomy or enclosed: Victor's workshop, Justine's prison cell, Victor's prison cell, the monster's hovel, the ship's cabins, the courtrooms.

3. These settings also link to certain **moods**. Exterior settings are places of refuge/retreat for the monster and Victor. Interior settings are usually places of psychological and/or physical captivity.

4. Some exterior settings are described as **sublime**: places of intense natural beauty and mystery.

5. Geneva, Victor's home, symbolises familiarity and civilisation, but is disrupted by William and Justine's murders.

What does Victor's workshop symbolise?

- Victor's separation from humanity and his need for privacy and secrecy.
- It is a place of horror and agony for Victor, even when empty. Clerval perceives Victor's **'dislike'** for the room and arranges a change of apartment.

How does Shelley use the Arctic?

- The Arctic symbolises a place of wonder and sublime beauty, testing the powers of human endurance.

- The monster's ability to thrive there contrasts with Victor's struggle to survive.
- It is the setting where the hunted (the monster) becomes the hunter.

What does Geneva symbolise?

- Geneva is Victor's home, symbolising love, familiarity and security.
- The city also represents Victor's past, particularly his childhood innocence.
- It is associated with Victor's family but becomes a place under threat.

How does Shelley use the De Lacey cottage and the hovel?

- The hovel is the monster's temporary refuge. The chink in the wall offers him illusory hope of acceptance by the De Laceys.
- The De Lacey's cottage represents both inclusion and exclusion. Safie is welcomed but the monster, seeking friendship, is ultimately rejected. It is the place where the monster tries but fails to cross into a world of human relationships.

Quick quiz

Answer these quick questions about setting and context.

1. What is galvanism?
2. What were the Luddites rioting about?
3. Who was Sir Humphrey Davy and what did he believe in?
4. When was the French Revolution?
5. What scientific terms were used about the relationship between life and death?
6. Give an example of a Romantic setting.
7. Give an example of a Gothic setting.
8. Give an example of a personal link which Shelley had with a) Romanticism and b) the Gothic.
9. What features characterise the interior settings in the novel?
10. What features characterise the exterior settings in the novel?

Power paragraphs

Choose one key **setting** or **context** related to the novel. Write **two paragraphs** explaining how Shelley makes use of this setting or context in relation to either a) theme or b) character.

CHARACTERS Victor Frankenstein

Five key things about Victor

1. **Victor** comes from a **relatively wealthy family** from **Geneva**. He is **loved by his family** and **friends** and admired by Robert Walton.
2. His **passion for learning** develops into an **unhealthy obsession**, isolating him from those he loves.
3. He can be seen as a tragic hero whose **flaws lead to his own** and **others' destruction**.
4. His **secret** makes him **unstable**, melancholic and revengeful.
5. By **the end**, **Victor** begins to **resemble the monster** he created.

What do we learn about Victor at the beginning of the novel?

- He has a privileged life, and enjoys his childhood with Elizabeth as a companion and Clerval as a friend.
- Hints of instability surface when he admits to a **'violent'** temper.
- His early scientific interest develops at Ingolstadt University. He makes **'rapid'** progress in his studies.
- His desire to create life involves him in sinister pursuits.

How does Victor change?

- Obsessiveness is a childhood trait, but Victor is protected at home. At Ingolstadt, his obsessions develop unchecked and damage his health. (Chapters 4–6)
- Two events, William's death and Justine's execution, intensify his guilt and misery and make him want revenge. (Chapters 7–9)
- Victor's emotions change from outrage to acceptance when the monster requests a mate. However, his ability to be 'moved' by the monster's needs is temporary. (Chapter 17)
- Victor considers the future, when making his second creation, something he did not do first time round. Nevertheless, his destruction of the monster's mate is brutal. (Chapter 20)
- Victor's thoughts begin to mimic the monster's. His dialogue with Walton near the end reveals his competing thoughts: he warns Walton about dangerous ambition but encourages him to hunt the monster. (Chapter 24)

Five key quotations

1. Victor's early memories about himself: 'Curiosity, earnest research to learn the hidden laws of nature, gladness akin to rapture' (Chapter 2)

2. Victor, imagining his future god-like status: 'A new species would bless me as its creator and source' (Chapter 4)

3. Victor's desire for revenge: 'the fiend that lurked in my heart' (Chapter 9)

4. Victor to the monster: 'There can be no community between you and me; we are enemies.' (Chapter 10)

5. Victor to Walton: 'Mine has been a tale of horrors' (Chapter 23)

Note it!

Victor is presented as much loved but his actions reveal him as a taker rather than a giver of love. He knows Elizabeth will marry him, despite warning her of a **'dreadful'** secret. He notices her waning **'vivacity'** but fails to recognise the reason why.

Exam focus

How can I write about Victor at the start of the novel? AO1

You can comment on how Shelley presents Victor as a child and adolescent.

At the start of the novel, Shelley presents Victor as a happy child, with a passion for learning. When Victor recalls his past he vividly remembers: 'Curiosity, earnest research to learn the hidden laws of nature, gladness akin to rapture'. The abstract nouns 'curiosity', 'gladness' and 'rapture' and the adjective 'earnest' all have positive, intensely pleasurable meanings. From Ingolstadt onwards Victor's feelings become predominantly negative but their intensity remains.	Topic sentence refers to specific point in novel
	Relevant quotation is fluently embedded
	Explores the language
	Summarises and moves the point on

Now you try!

Finish this paragraph about Victor's development later in the novel. Use one of the quotations from the list.

Shelley shows how Victor is deluded in his ambition to create life by....................................

My progress   Needs more work ☐   Getting there ☐   Sorted! ☐

CHARACTERS *The monster*

Five key things about the monster

1. The **monster** is **rejected by Victor** as soon as he is **given life**.
2. He **seeks out humans, learns their language**, but **generates** only **fear and horror** in them.
3. He **murders William** to have **revenge on Victor** and **sets up Justine as the killer** to make an **innocent person suffer like himself**.
4. He **murders Clerval and Elizabeth** after Victor **destroys** his **female mate**.
5. He **asks for forgiveness after Victor dies** and intends to **take his own life**.

What do we learn about the monster at the beginning of the novel?

- The monster finds Victor and tries to communicate with him.
- He secretly follows Victor and appears when Victor calls upon the spirit world. He silently communicates he is William's murderer. His second appearance is a direct confrontation, demanding that Victor listen to him.
- His story reveals his survival instincts and his eloquence with language.
- His desire to befriend and help others is misunderstood. He becomes the victim of people's prejudice.

How does the monster change?

- The monster changes from a non-verbal creature to a speaking being. (Chapters 11 and 12)
- His innocence and delight in nature contrasts with his misery among humans. His positive outlook is made negative by experience. (Chapters 11 and 13)
- He becomes irrationally revengeful, killing William to punish Victor, and framing Justine because she would never smile at him. This is payback for his psychological injuries. (Chapter 16)
- He refuses to accept isolation and demands a female companion (Chapter 17). Victor's betrayal leads him to murder Clerval and Elizabeth to make Victor's suffering equal to his own.
- Despite everything, he is sorrowful at Victor's death. He declares he will take his own life to avoid further emotional pain. (Walton, in continuation)

Five key quotations

1. The monster, by Victor's bedside: 'His jaws opened, and he muttered some inarticulate sounds, while a grin wrinkled his cheeks.' (Chapter 5)
2. Confronting Victor directly: 'I am thy creature' (Chapter 10)
3. Using **pathos** to tell his own story: 'Was I then a monster, a blot upon the earth … ?' (Chapter 13)
4. The monster, threatening Victor: 'if I cannot inspire love, I will cause fear' (Chapter 17)
5. After Victor's death: 'I shall ascend my funeral pile triumphantly' (Walton, in continuation)

Note it!

Shelley initially presents the monster as desiring a connection with his creator, Victor. Rejected, he desires fellowship with others. At the end, deprived of love and friendship, and with Victor dead, Shelley implies that taking his own life is the only means of control left to him.

Exam focus

How can I write about the monster at the start of the novel? AO1

You can comment on how Shelley presents the monster's desire to communicate.

At the beginning of the novel, Shelley shows the monster's desire to connect with Victor. Victor describes how 'he muttered some inarticulate sounds, while a grin wrinkled his cheeks'. The noun 'cheeks' suggest his origins as body parts and the verbs 'opened' and 'wrinkled' convey the mechanistic and grotesque nature of his actions. The monster's 'grin' seems horrifying, rather than friendly, and so reveals Victor's fear and misunderstanding.

Topic sentence refers to specific point in novel

Supports point with relevant quotation

Analyses Shelley's choice of language

Shows how the monster's intentions are misunderstood

Now you try!

Finish this paragraph about the monster's development. Use one of the quotations from the list.

Shelley shows how the monster learns to assert his power when he verbally threatens...

My progress   Needs more work ☐   Getting there ☐   Sorted! ☐   **35**

Five key things about Robert Walton

1. He is an **Arctic adventurer** whose **journey** coincides with Victor's.

2. The way he naturally **identifies** with **Victor's outlook** makes him the **ideal audience** for Victor.

3. His strong desire to **benefit mankind** by discovering **a passage to the North Pole** is similar to Victor's **desire** to discover the **secrets of life**.

4. His **ambition endangers** both **his life** and **his crew's** but, unlike Victor, he has the good sense to **turn back**.

5. He **challenges** the monster at the end about his **feelings** and **actions**.

What do we learn about Walton at the beginning of the novel?

- Walton writes letters to his sister, Margaret, expressing his Romantic attitude towards travel and discovery.

- He was an avid reader, had a **'neglected'** education and then tried unsuccessfully to become a poet. He was forbidden to pursue a **'seafaring life'**.

- He desires a friend to share and **'regulate'** his Romantic enthusiasms.

- The sighting of the monster excites his **'wonder'**. He is also astonished by Victor's question **'whither you are bound?'**

- His feelings of sympathy and compassion for Victor and the sharing of his own ambitions trigger the telling of Victor's story.

To what extent does Walton change?

- Walton's curiosity about the monster's **'formation'** suggests he hasn't fully appreciated the story's moral.

- In his final letters he is still motivated by success and ambition but eventually puts the crew's wellbeing first by reluctantly agreeing to turn the ship around.

- He shows courage and good judgement in delaying the monster's escape, but does not satisfy Victor's desire for revenge.

Five key quotations

1. Walton about the Arctic: 'it ever presents itself to my imagination as the region of beauty and delight' (Letter I)

2. Walton's wish for friendship: 'I desire the company of a man who could sympathise with me; whose eyes would reply to mine.' (Letter II)

3. Walton about Victor: 'I begin to love him as a brother' (Letter IV)

4. His responsibility to the crew: 'If we are lost, my mad schemes are the cause.' (Walton, in continuation)

5. Walton, meeting the monster: 'I approached this tremendous being' (Walton, in continuation)

Note it!

Initially, Shelley presents Walton as a Romantic figure full of dreams, passions and desires. But by the end, because of his difficult experience, he is realistic and clearer-sighted and perhaps more heroic.

Exam focus

How can I write about Walton at the start of the novel? AO1

You can comment on how Shelley presents Walton as a dreamer.

At the start of the novel, Shelley presents Walton as a Romantic. When describing his feelings about the Arctic, he writes: 'it ever presents itself to my imagination as the region of beauty and delight'. The abstract nouns 'imagination', 'beauty' and 'delight' are key Romantic ideas, expressing Walton's positive but slightly deluded thinking. His vision of the Arctic as a Romantic landscape reveals his partial understanding of nature's power which will, later, be modified by experience of its dangers.

Topic sentence refers to specific point in the novel

Relevant quotation is fluently embedded

Explains and analyses Shelley's choice of language

Moves the argument on

Now you try!

Finish this paragraph about Walton's development. Use one of the quotations from the list.

By the end of the novel, Walton reveals how his experiences have transformed his understanding of others when..............................

Five key things about Henry Clerval

1. Clerval is Victor's **closest friend** from **childhood**.
2. He **arrives** at the **university of Ingolstadt** just after **Victor has brought the monster to life**.
3. He **nurses** Victor back to **health** but is **not entrusted with Victor's secret**.
4. Clerval is a **foil** to Victor's character – a character **whose differences in outlook and actions contrast with the main character**.
5. Later, the **monster kills Clerval** in order to **punish Victor** for **destroying his female mate**.

What do we learn about Clerval at the beginning of the novel?

- Clerval is a merchant's son and is Victor's schoolfellow and closest friend.
- He enjoys reading heroic stories and hopes to live a courageous life, doing his best for others.
- His attendance at university is delayed because his father values trade above education.
- It is clear to Clerval that Victor is ill and he is curious to know the cause.
- He has a therapeutic influence on Victor, nursing him and suggesting the walking tour to aid his recovery.

What do we learn about Clerval as the novel progresses?

- He gently wins his father round about his education. (Chapters 3 and 5)
- Clerval places more importance on Victor's physical and mental health than his own needs. (Chapter 5)
- He acts as a go-between between Victor and his family to protect them. (Chapter 6)
- He uses the healing properties of literature as well as nature to support Victor's recovery. Later he shows great empathy over William's death. (Chapters 6 and 7)
- He sacrifices his ambition to travel to India to accompany Victor on a tour of Britain and makes the ultimate sacrifice with his life. (Chapters 19 and 21)

Five key quotations

1. As a child: 'He was a boy of singular talent and fancy.' (Chapter 2)
2. As a thwarted young man: 'Henry deeply felt the misfortune of being debarred from a liberal education.' (Chapter 3)
3. About Victor's ill-health: 'what, for God's sake, is the matter? ... How ill you are!' (Chapter 5)
4. His therapeutic effect: 'Study ... had rendered me unsocial; but Clerval called forth the better feelings of my heart' (Chapter 6)
5. The effect of his death: 'Clerval, my friend and dearest companion, had fallen a victim to me and the monster of my creation' (Chapter 21)

Note it!

Clerval's character does not change fundamentally for two reasons. First, he is the foil to Victor's character. Secondly, he is unaware of Victor's secret and so his friendship is not fully tested. Clerval remains his loyal and affectionate friend throughout.

Exam focus

How can I write about Clerval?

You can comment on how Clerval is presented as respectful and empathetic.

At the start of the novel, Shelley presents Clerval as a good friend, who treats people with love and respect. When Clerval is denied a university education, Victor comments, 'Henry deeply felt the misfortune of being debarred from a liberal education'. The phrase 'deeply felt' and the verb 'debarred' reveal both disappointment in and respect for his father's decision. At Ingolstadt, Clerval's concern for Victor is directly communicated by the comment: 'How ill you are!'

Topic sentence refers to specific point in the novel

Relevant quotation is fluently embedded

Explains in more detail

Analyses language

Now you try!

Finish this paragraph about the effect of Clerval on Victor. Use one of the quotations from the list.

Clerval's positive effect on Victor is shown ....

Three key things about Elizabeth

1. **Elizabeth is adopted** by the **Frankensteins** and is Victor's **'pretty present'**, **'cousin'** and wife-in-waiting.
2. She cares about others, e.g. **grieving for William** and **believing in Justine**.
3. She **marries Victor**. The **monster murders her** on the **wedding night**.

What is her function in the novel?

- She is a calm counter-balance to Victor's passion with her gentleness, empathy and thoughtfulness.
- She shows courage and loyalty, in pleading for Justine and marrying Victor, but falls victim to the monster.

Three key things about Justine

1. Justine is the **Frankensteins' servant** and treated as **part of the family**.
2. She is **Victor's 'great favourite'**, educated above her station and **close to Caroline**.
3. She is a **victim of injustice**, wrongly convicted and then **executed for William's murder**.

What is her function in the novel?

- When the monster plants the locket on Justine, it is a significant turning point. She innocently suffers the consequences of the monster's deeply felt injustice towards all humans.
- Her gratitude to the Frankensteins and courage highlight Victor's weakness.

Three key things about the Frankensteins

1. **Alphonse** is a **public figure in Geneva**. He **marries Caroline**, the orphan daughter of his poverty-stricken friend, and later **they adopt Elizabeth**.
2. With their **three sons, Victor, Ernest and William**, life is idyllic until Caroline's death from scarlet fever, caught from Elizabeth.
3. **William** is the **monster's 'first victim'**.

What is their function in the novel?

- Alphonse's actions and behaviour contribute to the **theme** of fatherhood.
- William symbolises the monster's desire for unprejudiced friendship. The revelation of William's identity and his terror trigger the monster's desire for revenge.

Three key quotations

1. Alphonse about Cornelius Agrippa: 'My dear Victor, do not waste your time upon this; it is sad trash.' (Chapter 2)

2. Victor about Caroline: 'On her death-bed the fortitude and benignity of this best of women did not desert her.' (Chapter 3)

3. William: '"monster! ugly wretch! you wish to eat me, and tear me to pieces"' (Chapter 16)

Note it!

Shelley explores themes of virtue, abandonment and sacrifice through female characters. Caroline, Elizabeth and Justine are all foundlings who become strong women. All, in different ways, die sacrificial deaths.

Exam focus

How can I write about Alphonse's character? AO1

You can comment on how Shelley uses Alphonse to communicate messages about fatherhood.

One of Alphonse's functions is to represent the responsibilities of fatherhood. Alphonse prefers gentle observation to direct intervention. This is evident when he discovers Victor reading Cornelius Agrippa: 'My dear Victor, do not waste your time upon this; it is sad trash'. The affectionate term of address 'My dear Victor' softens 'sad trash' which expresses mild criticism that Victor ignores. Alphonse's style of parenting is seen to have negative consequences.	Topic sentence introduces main idea
	Quotation carefully embedded
	Interpretation of the quotation
	Summarises and moves on the argument

Now you try!

Finish this paragraph about William. Use the appropriate quotation from the list.

As Victor's younger brother, Shelley uses William to express ....

CHARACTERS De Lacey, Felix, Agatha and Safie

Three key things about De Lacey

1. **De Lacey** is **old and blind**, a **loving father** to Agatha and Felix, and takes in Safie.
2. He is **poverty-stricken** and **exiled from Paris**, where he was **well-respected**.
3. He is **visited by the monster** and **recognises his 'sincerity'**.

What is his function in the novel?

- He acts as a counter-balance to all those horrified by the monster.
- He is a positive symbol of fatherhood, forgiving Felix, whose plot to help Safie's father caused the family's ruin. He is also the monster's ideal father-figure and protector.

Three key things about Agatha and Felix

1. **Felix** and Agatha are **De Lacey's affectionate children**. Both **go without so their father can eat**.
2. Agatha does domestic chores and Felix works outside. **Felix reads aloud to his father and Agatha**.
3. Both are **overjoyed at Safie's arrival. Felix is in love** with **Safie**.

What is their function in the novel?

- Their devotion to De Lacey symbolises positive child-parent relationships.
- Both show strength in dealing with adversity – a key theme.
- Their respect for each other and Safie highlights the monster's isolation.

Three key things about Safie

1. **Safie** is the daughter of a Turkish merchant, unjustly imprisoned in Paris. **Felix helps her to escape** but her **'treacherous' father takes her away**.
2. She later **escapes from her father**, showing her **independent spirit**.
3. She finds Felix and **her love and generosity** bring **joy to the De Laceys**.

What is her function in the novel?

- She represents cultural difference, her family having suffered oppression.
- Like the De Laceys, she is exiled and an outsider. Like the monster, she masters a new language but, unlike him, she is made welcome.

Four key quotations

1. De Lacey to the monster: 'I also am unfortunate; I and my family have been condemned, although innocent' (Chapter 15)

2. Agatha meeting Safie: 'the ever-gentle Agatha, kissed the hands of the lovely stranger' (Chapter 13)

3. Felix's protectiveness towards his father: 'Felix darted forward, and with supernatural force tore me from his father' (Chapter 15)

4. Safie's effect on the De Laceys: 'The presence of Safie diffused happiness' (Chapter 15)

Note it!

Shelley explores the theme of empathy in relation to the De Laceys. Their devotion to each other, warm welcome and continued delight in Safie provide the monster with an emotional education. So their later hostility to him is unbearable.

Exam focus

How can I write about Felix's character?

You can comment on how Shelley uses Felix to communicate a message about the strength of human love.

One of Felix's functions is to represent courage and protection. His reaction, on seeing the monster clinging to his father's knees, is to summon a 'supernatural force' to defend his father. He misunderstands what he sees and his primitive, animalistic response to danger, is highlighted by the verb 'tore'. Felix's love for his father overcomes any fear he might have.	Topic sentence introduces main idea
	Part of quotation carefully embedded
	Interpretation of the quotation and Felix's motivation

Now you try!

Finish this paragraph about Safie. Use one of the quotations from the list.

Shelley uses Safie to show how good...

1. Look at this ideas map about Victor. Is there anything else you could add?

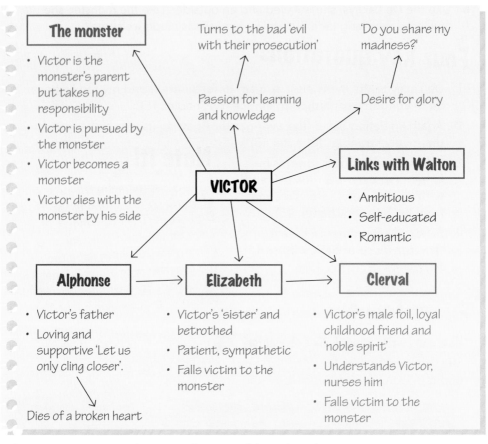

The monster

- Victor is the monster's parent but takes no responsibility
- Victor is pursued by the monster
- Victor becomes a monster
- Victor dies with the monster by his side

Turns to the bad 'evil with their prosecution'

'Do you share my madness?'

Passion for learning and knowledge

Desire for glory

VICTOR

Links with Walton

- Ambitious
- Self-educated
- Romantic

Alphonse

- Victor's father
- Loving and supportive 'Let us only cling closer'.

Dies of a broken heart

Elizabeth

- Victor's 'sister' and betrothed
- Patient, sympathetic
- Falls victim to the monster

Clerval

- Victor's male foil, loyal childhood friend and 'noble spirit'
- Understands Victor, nurses him
- Falls victim to the monster

2. Create your own ideas map for one of the other characters.

Quick quiz

Answer these quick questions about characters.

1. What kind of childhood did Victor have?
2. What happens when Victor goes to university in Ingolstadt?
3. Why does Victor agree to make a female mate for the monster and then destroy her?
4. What does Victor want from Walton at the end of the novel?

5. Why does the monster appear at Victor's bedside during the night following his 'birth'?
6. Why does the monster murder William?
7. Why does the monster go on to murder Clerval and Elizabeth?
8. What does the monster intend to do after Victor's death?
9. Who is Robert Walton and who is he writing to?
10. What feelings does Walton have about Victor?
11. What important decisions does Walton make at the end of the novel?
12. What kind of friend is Clerval?
13. What sacrifices does Clerval make for Victor?
14. Why and how does Clerval die?
15. What are Elizabeth's strengths?
16. Why is Justine found guilty and hanged for William's murder?
17. Who is in the extended family of the Frankensteins?
18. What kind of boy is William?
19. What does old De Lacey symbolise?
20. What effect does Safie have on the De Lacey household?

Power paragraphs

Write **a paragraph in response to each of these questions**. For each, try to **use one quotation** you have learned from this section.
1. In what ways is Clerval a character **foil** to Victor?
2. What are the similarities and differences between Walton and Victor?

Exam practice

Re-read the section in Chapter 9, from 'About this time' to 'had let loose among them?'

What does this extract tell you about Victor's behaviour and state of mind? Write **two paragraphs** explaining your ideas. You could comment on:
- Victor's motivation for taking out the boat on the lake
- what he thinks about when he is on the lake.

My progress   Needs more work ▢   Getting there ▢   Sorted! ▢   **45**

Five key things about the themes of knowledge and ambition

1. **Knowledge** is linked to **discovery**. Victor, Walton and the monster seek respectively to discover the **mystery of life**, the North Pole's **magnetic power** and of human **language** and **understanding**.

2. Desire for **knowledge** is a **'thirst'** for **Victor**, a **need** that must be satisfied.

3. Victor and Walton's **ambitions** are **self-centred**. The **monster's ambition**, to **develop relationships** with others, is more **humble**.

4. **Ambition** requires characters to **face physical** and **psychological** barriers.

5. **Knowledge** and **ambition** are shown to have **positive** and **negative** consequences.

What do knowledge and ambition mean and what are their effects?

- Knowledge is information and understanding gained by experience and education.

- Victor and Walton's pursuit of knowledge reflects antisocial ideas of excess and danger. The monster's knowledge reflects a desire for social connections.

- Ambition is a strong desire or yearning. Victor and Walton want to do extraordinary things. The monster's desire for a mate is more modest.

- Shelley examines the moral consequences of Victor and Walton's ambitions, which both endanger lives. Victor will not take responsibility for his creation, whereas Walton agrees to abandon his expedition.

How are the themes of knowledge and ambition woven into the narrative?

- Walton's expedition introduces and concludes the narrative.

- Victor's pursuit of scientific knowledge is key to his story.

- The monster's linguistic, moral and emotional knowledge is key to his story. Once he masters language, he realises that love, desire and prejudice characterise human relations.

- Victor and Walton's ambitions are fixed, whereas the monster's ambitions expand. All experience negative consequences after acquiring knowledge.

Five key quotations

1. Walton's ambition: 'the inestimable benefit which I shall confer on all mankind' (Letter I)

2. Victor's desire for knowledge: 'It was the secrets of heaven and earth that I desired to learn' (Chapter 2)

3. The monster's developing knowledge: 'Was man, indeed, at once so powerful, so virtuous and magnificent, yet so vicious and base?' (Chapter 13)

4. Victor to Walton on the dangers of ambition: 'I ardently hope that the gratification of your wishes may not be a serpent to sting you, as mine has been' (Letter IV)

5. The monster on the effect of painful knowledge: 'It clings to the mind, when it has once seized on it, like a lichen on the rock.' (Chapter 13)

Note it!

Victor's dying words express ambivalence towards ambition. First telling Walton to **'avoid ambition'** he then backtracks, saying **'Yet why do I say this?'** – questioning his own advice. Even as he dies, ideas about ambition retain some power over him.

Exam focus

How does Shelley explore knowledge and ambition? AO1

You can write about Victor's desire to create life.

Shelley explores the theme of knowledge and ambition through Victor's experience of creating the monster and dealing with the consequences. Victor's lofty ambition to create life is expressed as a desire to learn 'the secrets of heaven and earth'. 'Secrets' are usually not meant to be known and the phrase 'heaven and earth' implies that Victor is overreaching the powers of man. Shelley's choice of language makes the reader consider whether he should be trying to acquire it.

Clear topic sentence

Relevant fluently embedded quotation

Explores meaning

Links language and theme

Now you try!

Finish this paragraph about knowledge and ambition. Use one of the quotations from the list.

Shelley shows that some knowledge is difficult to accept when the monster ....

Five key things about nature and nurture

1. **Caroline** is **nurturing**, whereas **Alphonse** is **kind but more remote** and does not engage fully with Victor.

2. Victor uses **unnatural** means to **create life**. He likens the relationship to father/child but his feelings are closer to **godlike creator** than **nurturing father**.

3. Victor **rejects his creation**, considering him ugly and evil, and **denies** his **nurturing responsibility**.

4. The **monster** survives in **harmony with nature**, observing its effect on humans.

5. The **monster** believes he was **born naturally good** but **human society** has made him evil.

What does 'nature versus nurture' mean and how is it relevant?

- 'Nature versus nurture' is a debate about whether humans are most influenced by experience, upbringing and education or by certain genetically inherited traits.

- Victor is born into a benevolent family who moderate his behaviour. His passions lack control once he leaves home.

- The De Laceys live close to nature, away from civilisation. Their love for each other provides the monster's emotional education.

- The monster is content in nature when his basic needs are met. Once he learns language, he is exposed to ideas that erode his happiness.

How is the theme of nature and nurture woven into the narrative?

- Victor's upbringing and attachment to family and friends is the opening focus of his story.

- In Ingolstadt, away from family, Victor is oblivious to nature's **'charms'**.

- The monster seeking out Victor on his first night suggests a natural, child-like need for protection.

- De Lacey represents the ideal father, whose natural kindness is reciprocated by his children. This is why the monster is drawn to him.

- The monster's despair is rooted in his rejection. His attachment to Victor is still clear at the end.

Five key quotations

1. Victor's upbringing: 'I was ... their child, the innocent and helpless creature bestowed on them by Heaven' (Chapter 1)

2. Victor imagines his creation's thankfulness: 'No father could claim the gratitude of his child so completely as I should deserve theirs.' (Chapter 4)

3. The monster shows awareness of lack of nurture, using emotive language: 'No father had watched my infant days, no mother had blessed me with smiles' (Chapter 13)

4. Nature and nurture in the De Laceys: 'Felix carried with pleasure to his sister the first little white flower that peeped out' (Chapter 12)

5. The monster on nature versus nurture: 'I was benevolent and good; misery made me a fiend.' (Chapter 10)

Note it!

Nature and nurture are influences not be defied or avoided. In Ingolstadt Victor is 'insensible to nature' and avoids any family contact. Defying nature, by creating life from dead matter, and avoiding nurture, by rejecting the monster, both bring disaster.

Exam focus

How does Shelley explore nature and nurture? (AO1)

You can write about nature and nurture through Victor's relationship with the monster.

Shelley explores ideas of nature and nurture through Victor's relationship with the monster.	Topic sentence refers to theme
Victor fantasises about the 'gratitude' that his 'child' will feel but does not consider his own responsibilities or feelings.	Relevant quotation is fluently embedded
His egotism is suggested by the verbs 'claim' and 'deserve', revealing how he views fatherhood as an entitlement.	Explores meaning
Once alive, his unnatural creation fills him with disgust rather than joy.	Develops point

Now you try!

Finish this paragraph about nature and nurture. Use one of the quotations from the list.

Shelley shows the monster is aware of the awful effects of a lack of nurture when....

THEMES Companionship and isolation

Five key things about the themes of companionship and isolation

1. **Victor neither needs nor desires many friends** but values his **bonds** with Clerval. Victor's passion for reading implies **solitude**.
2. **Isolation** generates Walton's and the monster's **need for friendship**.
3. Walton, like Victor, **dislikes groups**. He spends his youth **'in solitude'** and is uncomfortable with the **'brutality'** of ship life.
4. Victor chooses to **isolate himself**, whereas the monster **is isolated**.
5. The monster is drawn towards the **companionable De Laceys**. After they reject him, his desire for a mate arises from a greater **need for acceptance**.

What are the effects of companionship and isolation?

- Companionship has positive associations: sharing, warmth, enjoyment and wellbeing.
- Isolation has negative associations of gloom and anxiety, generated by separation.
- Companionship has therapeutic effects. The De Laceys represent an ideal supportive family.

- Childhood companionship generates loyalty. Clerval and Elizabeth support Victor unconditionally.
- Isolation can be physical, emotional, voluntary or enforced. Victor moves away to work and the monster retreats for his own safety. Victor's secret isolates him, but the monster has to live alone.

How are companionship and isolation woven into the narrative?

- Walton desires friendship but is physically isolated. Victor is an ideal friend, an educated adventurer who can share Walton's enthusiasms.
- Victor is physically isolated at university and on the Orkneys. His secret and his tendency to withdraw isolate him emotionally.
- Elizabeth and Clerval are Victor's ideal companions. Both altruistic, they give more than they receive.
- The monster's story reveals the destructive consequences of extreme isolation and the denial of companionship and love.

Five key quotations

1. Victor's tendency to withdraw: 'It was my temper to avoid a crowd' (Chapter 2)
2. Walton's feelings of friendship towards Victor: 'I begin to love him as a brother' (Letter IV)
3. The monster's isolation: 'I am alone, and miserable; man will not associate with me' (Chapter 16)
4. The consequences of his isolation: 'My vices are the children of a forced solitude that I abhor' (Chapter 17)
5. The monster's view of the effects of companionship: 'my virtues will necessarily arise when I live in communion with an equal' (Chapter 17)

Note it!

Walton differentiates between companionship and friendship. He chooses a courageous crew but does not expect friendship. A similarity in education, manners and understanding is Walton's requirement for friendship. The monster hopes that equality between himself and his mate will lead to a deep friendship.

Exam focus

How does Shelley explore isolation?

You can write about how Shelley links isolation to misery.

Shelley explores the key theme of isolation through the monster's plight. The monster's understanding of the link between misery and isolation is expressed in the statement, 'I am alone and miserable; man will not associate with me'. His words poignantly summarise his alienation. The pronoun 'I' and the noun 'man' emphasise the rift he feels between himself and the human race.

Topic sentence refers to key theme	
Relevant quotation fluently embedded	
Tone evaluated	
Language explored and its effects	

Now you try!

Finish this paragraph about companionship. Use one of the quotations from the list.

The monster's understanding of the positive effects of companionship is revealed through his belief that ....

THEMES Prejudice

Five key things about the theme of prejudice

1. Several characters **experience prejudice**: the monster, Justine and Safie's parents.
2. The **justice system is prejudiced** in its treatment of **Justine** and **Safie's father**, both found **guilty** of crimes they did **not commit**. Victor is also **falsely accused** but, in his case, acquitted.
3. The monster is **pre-judged** on his **appearance**.
4. Safie's Turkish father **suffers prejudice** in Paris because of his **race**. Safie's mother, a **Christian Arab**, is enslaved in Turkey because of her **religion**.
5. There is **injustice** in Victor's prejudice against the monster. His **appearance, the cause of the prejudice**, is Victor's handiwork.

What does prejudice mean?

- Prejudice means a bias, an opinion not based on reason or knowledge. It is a barrier to understanding.
- Prejudice is linked with harm, hostility, victimisation, discrimination and injustice. It is associated with a group or society's power over an individual.
- Characters in the novel suffer the effects of prejudice or show prejudice.
- Prejudice is an emotional reaction. Shelley explores the extent to which it is instinctive or learned via experience or environment.

To what extent is prejudice overcome in the novel?

- Although Elizabeth believes in Justine's innocence, the judges and the crowd are prejudiced and the priest extracts a confession from her. The legal system, the church and public opinion override the truth.
- De Lacey's blindness frees him from prejudice based on appearance and allows him to sympathise with the monster. The family's misunderstanding of the monster means prejudice wins over tolerance.
- The monster succeeds in overcoming Victor's prejudice, persuading him to listen and make him a mate. Later, Victor's prejudice, based on fear, overrides his promise.
- Walton tries to control prejudice, linked to the monster's appearance, by shutting his eyes.

Five key quotations

1. Victor's prejudice based on the monster's looks: 'Oh! no mortal could support the horror of that countenance.' (Chapter 5)

2. The jury's prejudice against Justine: 'their settled conviction in the criminality of the saintly sufferer' (Chapter 8)

3. The monster on human prejudice – to De Lacey: 'a fatal prejudice clouds their eyes ... they behold only a detestable monster' (Chapter 15)

4. The monster's rationale for approaching William: 'this little creature was unprejudiced, and had lived too short a time to have imbibed a horror of deformity' (Chapter 16)

5. Walton's attempt to control prejudice: 'I shut my eyes ... to recollect what were my duties with regard to this destroyer.' (Walton, in continuation)

Note it!

Victor's prejudice against strangers' faces is explained by his early life of seclusion. Shelley suggests prejudice can arise from an unthinking preference for familiarity, generated by a limited exposure to difference.

Exam focus

How does Shelley explore prejudice?

You can write about how Shelley presents prejudice through the monster's encounters with humans.

Shelley explores the key theme of prejudice through the monster's developing understanding. He explains to De Lacey that the 'fatal' prejudice he suffers 'clouds' people's eyes, using an apt metaphor of visual impairment. His poetic language emphasises prejudice's devastating effect. Shelley's metaphor conveys the idea of prejudice's 'blindness'. It makes people see what they want to see, in this case, 'a detestable monster'.	Clear topic sentence
	Embedded quotation with analysis of imagery
	Theme conveyed via imagery
	Development of point

Now you try!

Finish this paragraph about another aspect of prejudice. Use one of the quotations from the list.

Shelley explores the way that prejudice is embedded in society in her description of the jury's verdict ....

My progress   Needs more work ☐   Getting there ☐   Sorted! ☐

Five key things about the themes of justice and revenge

1. **Alphonse** comes from a long line of **'syndics'** who administer the law and try to **enforce justice**. This suggests that **Victor** should **understand justice** through his **family background**.

2. Justine's death is a **miscarriage of justice**. Victor's silence, knowing Justine's innocence, is a **perversion of the course of justice**. These are different things.

3. The monster tries to **bring Victor to justice**, by **condemning** his behaviour.

4. **Injustice** generates the monster's **desire for revenge – a primitive form of justice** – to ensure Victor suffers too. Victor's desire for revenge is based on his perception of the monster's **'malice'**.

5. The monster **exacts his revenge** by setting up Justine and murdering William, Clerval and Elizabeth.

Why does the monster require justice and revenge?

- Justice means fair play, the opposite of prejudice. The monster suffers prejudice and seeks justice.

- Justice is concerned with respect for people's rights, rewarding those who merit justice and punishing those who do not. The monster takes justice into his own hands.

- Revenge is often the result of injustice. The monster takes revenge, trying to right the wrongs done to him.

How does the monster gain justice and revenge?

- The monster takes his opportunity to gain justice and revenge by murdering William and planting Elizabeth's locket on Justine.

- William's disclosure to the monster that he is a Frankenstein and a syndic's son provides the perfect circumstances for both revenge and justice.

- Clerval's and Elizabeth's murders are acts of revenge to make Victor feel guilt. The sense of justice is short-lived. The monster expresses regret for his actions to Walton.

Five key quotations

1. The monster's quest for justice from Victor: 'from you I ... seek that justice which I vainly attempted to gain from any other being' (Chapter 16)

2. Victor on the monster's request for a mate: 'justice ... demanded of me that I should comply with his request' (Chapter 17)

3. The monster after Felix's attack: 'my feelings were those of rage and revenge' (Chapter 16)

4. The monster to William: '"Frankenstein! you belong then to my enemy – to him towards whom I have sworn eternal revenge"' (Chapter 16)

5. The monster on the power of revenge: 'I was the slave, not the master, of an impulse, which I detested' (Walton, in continuation)

Note it!

There is symbolism in Justine's name which means morally right or fair. Despite her innocence, she sees **'no room for hope'** of acquittal due to the inexplicable circumstantial evidence. Victor describes her trial as a **'wretched mockery of justice'**.

Exam focus

How does Shelley explore the theme of revenge? (AO1)

You can write about how Shelley presents the monster's desire for revenge.

Shelley explores the theme of revenge through the De Laceys' rejection of the monster. Their unjust treatment generates feelings of 'rage and revenge' in the monster. The alliterative pairing intensifies these feelings, making them more resonant. Both are associated with violence and lack of control and mark a significant shift away from the emotional 'lessons' provided to the monster by the De Laceys.	Clear topic sentence
	Brief quotation fluently embedded
	Analyses language
	Develops point about theme

Now you try!

Finish this paragraph about justice. Use one of the quotations from the list.

Shelley shows that justice is associated with effort and difficulty when the monster eventually goes to..

1. Look at this ideas map representing the theme of nature. Is there anything else you could add?

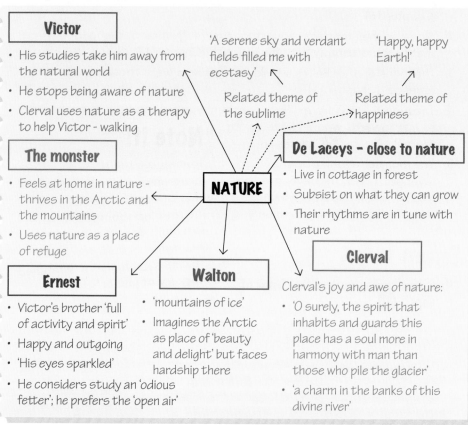

Victor

- His studies take him away from the natural world
- He stops being aware of nature
- Clerval uses nature as a therapy to help Victor - walking

The monster

- Feels at home in nature - thrives in the Arctic and the mountains
- Uses nature as a place of refuge

Ernest

- Victor's brother 'full of activity and spirit'
- Happy and outgoing
- 'His eyes sparkled'
- He considers study an 'odious fetter'; he prefers the 'open air'

Walton

- 'mountains of ice'
- Imagines the Arctic as place of 'beauty and delight' but faces hardship there

'A serene sky and verdant fields filled me with ecstasy'

'Happy, happy Earth!'

Related theme of the sublime

Related theme of happiness

NATURE

De Laceys - close to nature

- Live in cottage in forest
- Subsist on what they can grow
- Their rhythms are in tune with nature

Clerval

Clerval's joy and awe of nature:

- 'O surely, the spirit that inhabits and guards this place has a soul more in harmony with man than those who pile the glacier'
- 'a charm in the banks of this divine river'

2. Create your own ideas map for one of the other themes.

Quick quiz

1. Which themes do you associate with Walton's expedition?
2. Which characters do you associate with knowledge gained from reading?
3. Which characters have ambitions that endanger lives?
4. How do the images of a 'serpent' and 'lichen' link to the themes of ambition and knowledge?
5. Who defies nature and avoids nurture?

6. How does the story of Victor's parents' relationship and marriage link to the theme of nurture?

7. What is the unintended result of Victor's lack of superstition, which Alphonse nurtures in him as a child, when Victor is at Ingolstadt?

8. Which characters have a harmonious relationship with nature?

9. Which pairs or groups of characters make good companions in the novel?

10. What different types of isolation are represented in the novel?

11. What companion does the monster eventually think will best suit him?

12. What negative emotions are associated with isolation in the novel?

13. What different types of prejudice are illustrated in the novel?

14. Why does the monster think that William might be free of prejudice?

15. How is blindness linked to prejudice in the novel?

16. Why is Victor prejudiced against strangers?

17. Who is a 'slave' to revenge?

18. What is Alphonse's link to justice?

19. Whose trial is a 'mockery of justice'?

20. Who swears 'eternal revenge' on whom?

Power paragraphs

Write **a paragraph** in response to **each of these questions**. For each, try to **use one quotation** you have learned from this section.

1. How does Shelley link the monster with nature?
2. Why does Shelley choose a natural forest setting for the De Laceys?

Exam practice

Re-read the section in Chapter 4, from 'The dissecting room and the slaughterhouse' to 'should be completed'.

What is significant about Victor's relationship with nature here? Write **two paragraphs** explaining your ideas. You could comment on:

● Victor's unnatural work and how it isolates him from the natural world

● how Victor's neglect of nature goes hand in hand with neglect of his family.

LANGUAGE Imagery and vocabulary

Five key things about Shelley's use of imagery and vocabulary

1. Shelley uses **dynamic** imagery and lyrical language to **enhance** themes, such as knowledge and justice, and to **describe intense feelings** of misery and joy. Some images become motifs, such as **hands** and **the moon**.

2. She uses Gothic **imagery and vocabulary** to emphasise **negative feelings** and describe **violent events**.

3. She uses simile, metaphor and personification to heighten the reader's **understanding of characters, relationships** and **emotions**.

4. She uses **detailed vocabulary related to feelings** such as **'admiration'**, **'sympathy'**, **'compassion'** (positive); **'misery'**, **'despair'**, **'rage'** (negative) and an elegiac tone to highlight sadness and grief.

5. She uses **rhetorical techniques**: repetition, listing, questions, apostrophe and exclamatory sentences to animate each character's voice.

How does Shelley use imagery to create settings?

- Shelley uses pathetic fallacy to attribute human mood to settings, e.g. Victor's lift in mood in Chamonix: **'The very winds whispered in soothing accents'**.

- She uses Gothic imagery to create dramatic settings, e.g. the monster's sudden appearance: **'I saw, by the light of the moon, the daemon at the casement. A ghastly grin wrinkled his lips'**.

How does Shelley use simile and metaphor to construct character?

- Shelley describes characters' appearances, e.g. Elizabeth's hair is **'the brightest living gold'** seeming to **'set a crown of distinction on her head'**.

- She describes characters' actions, e.g. the monster says to Victor **'I will watch you with the wiliness of a snake'**.

How does Shelley use rhetorical techniques to create impact?

- Shelley uses rhetorical questions to explore the monster's mind, e.g. **'What did this mean? Who was I? What was I?'**

- She uses superlatives and lists for emphasis, e.g. Clerval: **'"I have seen ... the most beautiful scenes ... I have seen this lake agitated by a tempest"'**.

Five key quotations

1. Simile: Alphonse's protectiveness towards Caroline: 'He strove to shelter her, as a fair exotic is sheltered by a gardener' (Chapter 1)

2. Metaphor: Victor's despair: 'But I am a blasted tree; the bolt has entered my soul' (Chapter 19)

3. Contrast used for emphasis by the monster: 'if I cannot inspire love, I will cause fear' (Chapter 17)

4. Exclamatory sentences: animating the monster's dialogue: 'Oh, Frankenstein! generous and self-devoted being!' (Walton, in continuation)

5. Motifs to reinforce plot: 'the print of the murderer's finger was on his neck' (Chapter 7); 'the black mark of fingers on his neck' (Chapter 21)

Note it!

Using imagery from Milton's 'Paradise Lost', based on the biblical story of Adam and Eve, Shelley has the monster describe himself as the serpent: **'God, in pity, made man beautiful and alluring, after his own image; but my form is a filthy type of yours'**.

Exam focus

How can I write about Shelley's use of imagery? (AO2)

You can explore how imagery conveys intense feelings.

Shelley explores the theme of despair through powerful imagery.	Topic sentence links imagery to theme
Victor compares himself to a tree struck by lightning: 'But I am a blasted tree; the bolt has entered my soul'.	Embedded quotations
The metaphor is a Gothic image of destruction and the second simple statement poignantly describes Victor's weakened spirit.	Detailed language analysis
Through imagery Shelley conveys intensity of feeling and how Victor sees himself as marked out.	Summarises effect of imagery

Now you try!

Finish this paragraph about the use of exclamatory sentences. Use one of the quotations from the list.

At the end, Shelley uses exclamatory sentences when the monster expresses..........

My progress   Needs more work ☐   Getting there ☐   Sorted! ☐   59

Five key things about Shelley's use of narrators

1. Shelley uses **three** first-person narrators, Walton, Victor and the monster.
2. These **different narrative** voices reflect different life experiences and values.
3. She uses **different narrative** perspectives to tell the story from different viewpoints.
4. These perspectives help the reader understand how each narrator thinks and feels.
5. Shelley allows the reader to feel **sympathy** and antipathy towards the narrators.

How does Shelley vary her style to suit the different narrators?

- Shelley uses Romantic language for Walton in the opening letters, similar to Victor's, e.g. **'I feel my heart glow with an enthusiasm which elevates me to heaven.'**
- Victor's language is often excessive, e.g. **'I trod heaven in my thoughts, now exulting in my powers, now burning with the idea of their effects.'**
- Shelley uses eloquent, reasoned and persuasive language for the monster, often addressed to Victor, e.g. **'Unfeeling, heartless creator! You had endowed me with perceptions and passions and then cast me abroad.'**

How does Shelley use language to create different voices?

- Shelley uses exclamations, leading questions and metaphor to show emotional turmoil, e.g. in Victor's words to Walton: **'Unhappy man! Do you share my madness? Have you drank also of the intoxicating draught?'**
- Assertive language, such as the verb 'must', is used to add persuasion to the monster's words, e.g. **'My companion must be of the same species, and have the same defects. This being you must create.'**
- She uses the language of reason to create emotional distance, e.g. in Walton's words to the monster: **'If you had listened to the voice of conscience, and heeded the stings of remorse ... Frankenstein would yet have lived.'**

Five key quotations

1. Walton's reasoning about the crew's request: 'Yet could I, in justice, or even in possibility, refuse this demand?' (Walton, in continuation)

2. Victor's egotism about Justine's suffering: 'The tortures of the accused did not equal mine' (Chapter 8)

3. The monster's naivety about the De Laceys: 'I longed to discover the motives and feelings of these lovely creatures' (Chapter 12)

4. Victor's rhetoric to Walton's crew: 'What do you demand of your captain? Are you then so easily turned from your design?' (Walton, in continuation)

5. The monster's declaration to Victor: 'Blasted as thou wert, my agony was still superior to thine' (Walton, in continuation)

Note it!

The monster's language is at times old-fashioned or archaic, e.g. using the pronouns 'thou' and 'thine', instead of 'you' and 'yours' and verbs like 'wert' instead of 'were'. These imply that his language is partly shaped by his reading of old texts. This gives him a distinctive voice.

Exam focus

How can I write about Shelley's use of multiple voices? (AO2)

You can write about the links between the narrative voices.

Shelley uses multiple narrators to show similarities and differences in characters' thinking.	Topic sentence on uses of multiple narration
Victor claims his suffering is worse than Justine's and that 'her tortures' 'did not equal' his.	Clear evidence
He uses the language of measurement, 'not equal', to compare their suffering and by ending with the pronoun 'mine', reveals his egotism.	Analysis of specialist language
The monster tells the dead Victor his own 'agony' is 'superior to thine', echoing the same idea.	Develops point about similarity

Now you try!

Finish this paragraph about Walton's narrative voice. Use one of the quotations from the list.

At the end of the novel, when Walton faces the crew's revolt, he questions himself with ....

Five key things about the exam

1. You will have **one** question on *Frankenstein* which will be based on a **passage** given to you on the exam paper.
2. It will focus on **Shelley's presentation** of an aspect of the novel, such as a **character**, **relationship** or a **theme**.
3. You will have about **45–50 minutes** to read and respond to the question.
4. The question is worth **30 marks**.
5. The question assesses **AOs 1, 2 and 3**. Remember that **AO3** relates to **context**.

What will a question look like?

1. Starting with this extract, how does Shelley present the character of Justine?

   Write about:
   - how Shelley presents Justine in this extract
   - how Shelley presents Justine in the novel as a whole.

   [30 marks]

> You must refer to the given passage

> You must explain the techniques Shelley uses

> This is the area you must tackle

> A reminder to begin with the given passage/ extract

> A reminder to **also** write about the whole of the novel

Do all questions look the same?

- Not all questions will begin this way. Some might contain statements or questions that require you to consider 'how far' a character deserves, for example, sympathy or admiration. For example, **'Starting with this extract, how far does Shelley present the monster as a character to be admired?'**
- Not all questions will be about a single character. Some might ask you about a **relationship** between two characters, e.g. between Victor and Walton.

What do I need to do to get a good mark?

Use this grid to understand what your current level is and how to improve it:

	AO1 Read, understand, respond	**AO2** Analyse language, form, structure and effects	**AO3** Show understanding of contexts
High	• You make **precise references** to the **passage** and *Frankenstein* **as a whole**. • Your argument is **well-structured**, with quotations **fluently embedded** in sentences. • You cover **both** the extract and the whole novel.	• You **analyse** and **interpret** the methods Shelley uses **very effectively**. • You **explore thoughtfully** the effects of these on the reader. • You show **excellent use** of subject terminology.	• You make **detailed, relevant links** between specific elements of the novel and social and historical contexts.
Mid	• You make a **range of references** to the passage and the novel as a whole. • You respond in **a clear, logical way** with **relevant** quotations chosen.	• You **explain clearly** some of the methods Shelley uses, and **some effects** on the reader. • You use **mostly relevant** subject terminology.	• You show **clear evidence** of understanding context which is **linked** to the novel in places.
Lower	• You make **some references** to the passage and novel as a whole, but in rather a **patchy** way. • You make **some useful points** but evidence is **not always clear or relevant**.	• You make **occasional attempts** to explain Shelley's methods but these are a little **unclear**. • You show **some use** of subject terminology.	• You demonstrate **basic awareness** of context but **links** to the novel are **undeveloped** and **not always relevant**.

Read this exam-style character question

Read this extract from Chapter 8 in which Victor describes a visit he makes with Elizabeth to see Justine in prison after she has made a false confession. Then answer the question that follows.

> During this conversation I had retired to the corner of the prison-room, where I could conceal the horrid anguish that possessed me. Despair! Who dared talk of that? The poor victim, who on the morrow was to pass the awful boundary between life and death, felt not as I did, such deep and bitter agony. I
> 5 gnashed my teeth, and ground them together, uttering a groan that came from my inmost soul. Justine started. When she saw who it was, she approached me, and said, 'Dear sir, you are very kind to visit me; you, I hope, do not believe that I am guilty?'
> I could not answer. 'No, Justine,' said Elizabeth, 'he is more convinced of your innocence than I was; for even when he heard that you had confessed, he
> 10 did not credit it.'
> 'I truly thank him. In these last moments I feel the sincerest gratitude towards those who think of me with kindness. How sweet is the affection of others to such a wretch as I am! It removes more than half of my misfortune; and I feel as if I could die in peace, now that my innocence is acknowledged by
> 15 you, dear lady, and your cousin.'
> Thus the poor sufferer tried to comfort others and herself. She indeed gained the resignation she desired. But I, the true murderer, felt the never-dying worm alive in my bosom, which allowed of no hope or consolation. Elizabeth also wept, and was unhappy; but hers also was the misery of innocence, which, like a cloud that passes over the fair moon, for a while hides
> 20 but cannot tarnish its brightness. Anguish and despair had penetrated into the core of my heart; I bore a hell within me, which nothing could extinguish.

2. Starting with this extract, explore how far Shelley presents Victor as someone to be pitied. Write about:
   - how Shelley presents Victor's character in the extract
   - how far Victor is a character to be pitied in the novel as a whole.

[30 marks]

Read this extract from Chapter 7 in which Alphonse writes to Victor about William's death and the family's grief. Then answer the question that follows.

About five in the morning I discovered my lovely boy, whom the night before I had seen blooming and active in health, stretched on the grass livid and motionless: the print of the murderer's finger was on his neck.

He was conveyed home, and the anguish that was visible in my
5 countenance betrayed the secret to Elizabeth. She was very earnest to see the corpse. At first I attempted to prevent her; but she persisted, and entering the room where it lay, hastily examined the neck of the victim, and clasping her hands exclaimed, "O God! I have murdered my darling child!"

She fainted, and was restored with extreme difficulty. When she again lived,
10 it was only to weep and sigh. She told me that that same evening William had teased her to let him wear a very valuable miniature that she possessed of your mother. This picture is gone, and was doubtless the temptation which urged the murderer to the deed. We have no trace of him at present, although our exertions to discover him are unremitted; but they will not restore my beloved
15 William!

Come, dearest Victor; you alone can console Elizabeth. She weeps continually and accuses herself unjustly as the cause of his death; her words pierce my heart. We are all unhappy; but will not that be an additional motive for you, my son, to return and be our comforter? Your dear mother! Alas,
20 Victor! I now say, Thank God she did not live to witness the cruel, miserable death of her youngest darling!

Come, Victor; not brooding thoughts of vengeance against the assassin, but with feelings of peace and gentleness, that will heal, instead of festering, the wounds of our minds. Enter the house of mourning, my friend, but with
25 kindness and affection for those who love you, and not with hatred for your enemies.

Your affectionate and afflicted father,
ALPHONSE FRANKENSTEIN

3. Starting with this extract, how does Shelley present the character of Alphonse?

Write about:

● how Shelley presents the character of Alphonse in this extract
● how Shelley presents the character of Alphonse in the novel as a whole.

[30 marks]

EXAM PRACTICE Planning your character response

Five key stages to follow

1. **Read** the **question**; **highlight** the key words.
2. **Read** the **passage** with the **key words** from the **question** in mind.
3. Quickly **generate ideas** for your response.
4. **Plan** for paragraphs.
5. **Write** your response; **check it** against your plan as you progress.

What do I focus on?

Highlight the **key words**:

2. Starting with this extract, explore how Shelley presents Victor as someone to be pitied. Write about:
   ● how Shelley presents Victor's character in this extract
   ● how far Shelley presents Victor as a character to be pitied in the novel as a whole. **[30 marks]**

What do they tell you? Focus on extract and whole text; explain the specific methods Shelley uses; stick to topic – Victor as a character to be pitied.

How should I read the passage?

● Check for any immediate links to the question (e.g. his feelings of agony).
● Look for any evidence/quotations you could highlight (e.g. **'a groan that came from my inmost soul'**).

How do I get my ideas?

Note your ideas in a spider diagram or list them in a table:

The extract

Contrast – Victor's pitiable behaviour versus Elizabeth and Justine's composure

Victor's loss of control: 'I gnashed my teeth'

Victor as a character to be pitied

The novel as a whole

Victor cruel to monster: 'Begone vile insect'

Thoughtless about others: 'They hardly know how ill you have been, and are uneasy at your long silence.'

How do I structure my ideas?

Make a **plan** for **paragraphs.*** Decide the order for your points:

- Paragraph 1: *Go straight into your first point. Victor is full of self-pity in the extract. The reader may or may not feel pity for him. They may feel anger. Self-pity is characteristic of Victor throughout the novel.*

- Paragraph 2: *Victor's agony – Faustian imagery is contrasted with Elizabeth and Justine's composure. Shelley describes Victor's mind but presents Elizabeth and Justine through direct speech.*

- Paragraph 3: *Victor sees their sorrow but believes his own is worse: 'never-dying worm' Gothic metaphor.*

- Paragraph 4: *Victor's behaviour in novel as a whole. Lack of pity for monster. Thoughtless towards Elizabeth and Alphonse. Others pity him without understanding his situation/knowing his secret. Hard for reader to pity him.*

- Paragraph 5: *Walton admires and pities Victor. Walton and the monster are distressed by Victor's death. How novel closes. Walton's feelings help sway reader's sympathy towards Victor.*

How do I write effectively?

Write **clear**, **analytical** paragraphs and **embed** your evidence fluently, e.g.

In the extract, Shelley presents Victor as full of self-pity. How far a reader feels pity for his 'deep and bitter agony' will depend on whether they feel sympathy for his situation or anger at his ego. Victor, understandably, is in 'anguish and despair' because of William's murder and the injustice of Justine's situation. Nevertheless, his tendency to see his own misery as worse is clearly presented by Shelley here and in the novel as a whole.	Main point: extract
	Uses key words from question
	Quotations are well embedded
	Links point to rest of novel
	Summary point

Now you try!

Re-read Question 3 on page 65 and plan your response in the same way.

*The plan above and the sample answers on pages 68 and 70 have five paragraphs, but you don't need to be limited to this if you have more points to include.

What does a Grade 5 answer look like?

Read the task again, then the sample answer below.

2. Starting with this extract, explore how Shelley presents Victor as someone to be pitied.

    Write about:
    - how Shelley presents Victor's character in this extract
    - how Shelley presents Victor as a character to be pitied in the novel as a whole.   **[30 marks]**

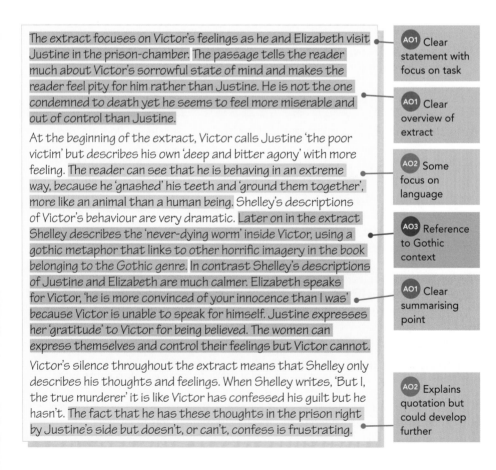

The extract focuses on Victor's feelings as he and Elizabeth visit Justine in the prison-chamber. The passage tells the reader much about Victor's sorrowful state of mind and makes the reader feel pity for him rather than Justine. He is not the one condemned to death yet he seems to feel more miserable and out of control than Justine.

> **AO1** Clear statement with focus on task

> **AO1** Clear overview of extract

At the beginning of the extract, Victor calls Justine 'the poor victim' but describes his own 'deep and bitter agony' with more feeling. The reader can see that he is behaving in an extreme way, because he 'gnashed' his teeth and 'ground them together', more like an animal than a human being. Shelley's descriptions of Victor's behaviour are very dramatic. Later on in the extract Shelley describes the 'never-dying worm' inside Victor, using a gothic metaphor that links to other horrific imagery in the book belonging to the Gothic genre. In contrast Shelley's descriptions of Justine and Elizabeth are much calmer. Elizabeth speaks for Victor, 'he is more convinced of your innocence than I was' because Victor is unable to speak for himself. Justine expresses her 'gratitude' to Victor for being believed. The women can express themselves and control their feelings but Victor cannot.

> **AO2** Some focus on language

> **AO3** Reference to Gothic context

> **AO1** Clear summarising point

Victor's silence throughout the extract means that Shelley only describes his thoughts and feelings. When Shelley writes, 'But I, the true murderer' it is like Victor has confessed his guilt but he hasn't. The fact that he has these thoughts in the prison right by Justine's side but doesn't, or can't, confess is frustrating.

> **AO2** Explains quotation but could develop further

Victor is pitied by other characters in the novel as a whole. His friend Clerval is very caring when he visits Victor in Ingolstadt and does everything he can to help Victor get better, including the Romantic idea of the healing power of nature. Elizabeth also loves Victor very much and is full of pity when she sees how ill he is. Victor seems to be very much loved and pitied by his family and friends even though he does little to earn their love and pity. He does not pity the monster and abandons him. It is hard to feel pity for Victor because the reader knows how much he has hurt the monster, through the monster's own narration, and feels Victor should take more responsibility for his actions.

Paragraph 4

Victor is a man who is both admired and pitied by Walton who wants to be his friend. Walton, a man of adventure, looks up to Victor and his 'tears flow' when Victor dies. Walton, as the framing narrator, is given an important position by Shelley so his emotional response to Victor and his story help sway the reader's sympathy for Victor at the end.

Paragraph 5

Check the skills

Re-read paragraphs four and five of this response and:

- highlight other **points** made
- circle any reference to **context**
- underline any places where the student has made an **interpretation**.

Now you try!

Look again at paragraph three (*'Victor's silence throughout the extract …'*, etc.) and improve it by:

- Adding a **reference or quotation** about Victor being silent and withdrawn from another part of the novel to emphasise this character trait
- **Explaining** why Victor's inability to confess is frustrating
- Ending with a **summary point** about pity the reader might or might not feel towards Victor
- Improving the overall **style** by making sure your sentences **flow**; using **connectives** to **link** ideas

What does a Grade 7+ answer look like?

Read the task again, then the sample answer below.

2. Starting with this extract, explore how Shelley presents Victor as a character to be pitied.

Write about:

- how Shelley presents Victor's character in this extract
- how Shelley presents Victor as a character to be pitied in the novel as a whole. **[30 marks]**

In the extract, Shelley presents Victor as full of self-pity, a characteristic trait throughout the novel. How far a reader feels pity for his 'deep and bitter agony' will depend on whether they feel sympathy for his situation or anger at his ego. Victor is in despair because of William's murder and the injustice of Justine's situation. Nevertheless, his tendency to see his misery as worse is presented when he exclaims, 'Despair! Who dared talk of that?'

AO1 Focus on key question words, 'how far'

AO3 Good use of context linked to characterisation

Shelley shows the workings of Victor's tormented mind – reminiscent of Marlowe's mythic Dr Faustus. His gnashing and grinding of teeth, and the 'groan' from his 'inmost soul' suggest this, as does the dramatic contrast between his pitiful behaviour and the female characters' composure. Elizabeth claims beforehand that she cannot visit Justine alone. In reality, Victor offers her no support as he is rendered speechless by his despair and isolates himself. Shelley uses direct speech to enable Elizabeth to speak eloquently on Victor's behalf and for Justine to express her concern.

AO2 Carefully selected evidence

AO1 Excellent textual knowledge

AO2 Analysis of literary device and effect

Victor's downplaying of their suffering might provoke frustration rather than pity. Victor's self-obsession limits his empathy. He sees Justine as 'the poor sufferer' and comments on Elizabeth's 'misery', suggesting some emotional awareness, but he diminishes their feelings as the 'misery of innocence'. The simile of a cloud covering the moon implies their temporary misery and the permanence of his own. Shelley also uses two disturbing Gothic metaphors to intensify Victor's horrified mind-state; the 'never-dying worm' and the 'hell within'.

AO2 Fluent introduction of new aspect to analyse

AO3 Gothic context neatly integrated

Throughout the novel, Victor often shows a lack of compassion, such as his heartless treatment of the monster and his thoughtless neglect of Elizabeth. This trait and his failure to consider the consequences of his Faustian ambition are presented as significant character flaws, affecting the reader's emotional response to him. Clerval, Elizabeth and Alphonse remain loyal, although ignorant of the cause of Victor's misery. That Victor does not share his secret with anyone, apart from Walton, could inspire pity for his psychological burden. His decision, however, to tell Elizabeth after they are married could be interpreted as calculating and patriarchal. Victor instructs Elizabeth not to 'mention' or 'allude' to the secret and these terms remain unquestioned.

— Paragraph 4

Walton seems to have the final say on whether Victor deserves pity when he writes to his sister, 'What can I say that will enable you to understand the depths of my sorrow?' His wording anticipates her probable confusion. Walton hears the monster's 'suffocated' voice at Victor's death and it is Walton's pity for the monster, rather than Victor, that has the final word.

— Paragraph 5

Check the skills

Re-read paragraphs four and five of this response and:
- identify any particularly **fluent** or **well-expressed** ideas
- find any further references to **context**
- highlight any places where the student has shown **deeper insight** and offered **original** or particularly **thoughtful** ideas or made interesting **links**.

Now you try!

Now, using the plan you made for Question 3 on page 67, write a full response. Here's a reminder of the question:

3. Starting with this extract, how does Shelley present the character of Alphonse? Write about:
   - how Shelley presents the character of Alphonse in this extract
   - how Shelley presents the character of Alphonse in the novel as a whole.

   [30 marks]

- Try to match your answer to the High Level objectives on page 63.

Read this exam-style theme question

Read this extract from Chapter 2 in which Victor describes his childhood. Then answer the question that follows.

> We possessed a house in Geneva, and a *campagne* on Belrive, the eastern shore of the lake, at the distance of rather more than a league from the city. We resided principally in the latter, and the lives of my parents were passed in considerable seclusion. It was my temper to avoid a crowd, and to attach
> 5 myself fervently to a few. I was indifferent, therefore, to my schoolfellows in general; but I united myself in the bonds of the closest friendship to one among them. Henry Clerval was the son of a merchant of Geneva. He was a boy of singular talent and fancy. He loved enterprise, hardship, and even danger, for its own sake. He was deeply read in books on chivalry and
> 10 romance. He composed heroic songs, and began to write many a tale of enchantment and knightly adventure. He tried to make us act plays, and to enter into masquerades, in which the characters were drawn from the heroes of Roncesvalles, of the Round Table of King Arthur, and the chivalrous train who shed their blood to redeem the holy sepulchre from the hands of the
> 15 infidels.
>
> No human being could have passed a happier childhood than myself. My parents were possessed by the very spirit of kindness and indulgence. We felt that they were not the tyrants to rule our lot according to their caprice, but the agents and creators of all the many delights which we enjoyed. When I
> 20 mingled with other families, I distinctly discerned how peculiarly fortunate my lot was, and gratitude assisted the development of filial love.
>
> My temper was sometimes violent, and my passions vehement; but by some law in my temperature they were turned not towards childish pursuits but to an eager desire to learn.

4. Starting with this extract, how does Shelley present the importance of childhood in the novel? Write about:
   - how Shelley presents the importance of childhood in this extract
   - how Shelley presents the importance of childhood in the novel as a whole.

[30 marks]

Now read this further theme question

Read this extract from Chapter 6 in which Clerval and Victor go on a walking tour. Then answer the question that follows.

> Henry proposed a pedestrian tour in the environs of Ingolstadt, that I might bid a personal farewell to the country I had so long inhabited. I acceded with pleasure to this proposition: I was fond of exercise, and Clerval had always been my favourite companion in the rambles of this nature that I had taken
> 5 among the scenes of my native country.
>   We passed a fortnight in these perambulations: my health and spirits had long been restored, and they gained additional strength from the salubrious air I breathed, the natural incidents of our progress, and the conversation of my friend. Study had before secluded me from the intercourse of my fellow-
> 10 creatures, and rendered me unsocial, but Clerval called forth the better feelings of my heart; he again taught me to love the aspect of nature, and the cheerful faces of children. Excellent friend! how sincerely did you love me, and endeavour to elevate my mind until it was on a level with your own! A selfish pursuit had cramped and narrowed me, until your gentleness and affection
> 15 warmed and opened my senses; I became the same happy creature who, a few years ago, loved and beloved by all, had no sorrow or care. When happy, inanimate nature had the power of bestowing on me the most delightful sensations. A serene sky and verdant fields filled me with ecstasy. The present season was indeed divine; the flowers of spring bloomed in the hedges,
> 20 while those of summer were already in bud. I was undisturbed by thoughts which during the preceding year had pressed upon me, notwithstanding my endeavours to throw them off, with an invincible burden.
>   Henry rejoiced in my gaiety, and sincerely sympathised in my feelings: he exerted himself to amuse me, while he expressed the sensations that filled
> 25 his soul.

5. Starting with this extract, how does Shelley present the relationship between nature and nurture? Write about:

- how Shelley presents the relationship between nature and nurture in this extract
- how Shelley presents the relationship between nature and nurture in the novel as a whole.

[30 marks]

Five key stages to follow

1. **Read** the **question**; **highlight** key words.
2. **Read** the **passage** with the **key words** from the **question** in mind.
3. Quickly **generate ideas** for your response.
4. **Plan** for paragraphs.
5. **Write** your response; **check it** against your plan as you progress.

What do I focus on?

Highlight the **key words**:

> 4. Starting with this extract, how does Shelley present the importance of childhood in the novel? Write about:
>   - how Shelley presents the importance of the theme of childhood in this extract
>   - how Shelley presents the importance of the theme of childhood in the novel as a whole. **[30 marks]**

What do they tell you? Focus on extract and whole text; explain the specific methods Shelley uses; stick to topic – the importance of childhood.

How should I read the passage?

- Check for any immediate links to the question (e.g. Victor's childhood is recalled, where he was born, his friendship with Clerval).
- Look for any evidence/quotations you could highlight (e.g. **'No human being could have passed a happier childhood than myself'**).

How do I get my ideas?

Note your ideas in a spider diagram or list them in a table:

The extract
Victor to Walton: happy memories – a good childhood is one nurtured by parents; 'kindness and indulgence'

Friendship with Clerval also significant

The novel as a whole
Other childhoods are lacking: Caroline and Elizabeth described as 'an orphan and a beggar'

Justine: 'her mother could not endure her'

> The importance of childhood

74

How do I structure my ideas?

Make a **plan** for **paragraphs**.* Decide the order for your points:

- Paragraph 1: *Victor's happy childhood nostalgically evoked when talking to Walton. It contrasts with several deprived ones, involving poverty, vulnerability and rejection. Ideal versus reality.*

- Paragraph 2: *Extract refers to two homes; privilege, privacy and seclusion. Victor does not needs many friends but Clerval very important. His childhood focus around imaginative play and time spent with Clerval – a 'Romantic' child.*

- Paragraph 3: *Extract is reflective, idealising childhood. Vital bonds of family and friendship forged. Tone is a mixture of pride and sadness.*

- Paragraph 4: *Elizabeth, Justine's and Caroline's negative early childhoods and the Monster's early days all contrast with Victor's nurtured childhood. Early deprivation does not always lead to later difficulties but does in the monster's case. Filial gratitude. Wider cultural debate about childhood.*

- Paragraph 5: *Childhood a key theme explored through major and minor characters. Shelley raises questions and explores: vulnerability in childhood, significance of nurture, dangers of indulgence, effects of neglect.*

How do I write effectively?

Write **clear**, **analytical** paragraphs and **embed** your evidence fluently, e.g.

In the extract, Shelley presents childhood through Victor's nostalgia. Telling Walton his life story from this perspective of lost innocence influences his narration. He emphasises that 'No human being could have passed a happier childhood', thus painting an idyllic picture. Yet in the novel as a whole, childhood is associated with vulnerability. Some characters, including the monster, have 'parents' unable, or unwilling, to look after them, which contrasts sadly with Victor's upbringing.	Overview point – extract
	Key term
	Quotations are well embedded
	New point also links to rest of novel
	Summarising point

Now you try!

Re-read Question 5 on page 73 and plan your response in the same way.

*The plan above and the sample answers on pages 76 and 78 have five paragraphs, but you don't need to be limited to this if you have more points to include.

What does a Grade 5 answer look like?

Read the task again, then the sample answer below.

4. Starting with this extract, how does Shelley present the importance of childhood in the novel? Write about:
- how Shelley presents the importance of the theme of childhood in this extract
- how Shelley presents the importance of the theme of childhood in the novel as a whole. **[30 marks]**

The extract deals with Victor's memories of childhood. He is telling Walton about his life and begins with his upbringing. He is wealthy and his childhood was happy. Shelley shows how Victor's childhood was important to him and that he realises he was lucky. However, in the novel as a whole childhood does not have such a positive presentation and several characters experience sadness and hardship. The theme recurs throughout the novel.

> **AO1** Clear statement sets out scope of theme

> **AO1** Clear progression of theme to whole novel

At the beginning of the extract Victor describes where he lived, mentioning that his family had two homes, one in the city of Geneva and the other a 'campagne', a house in the countryside. He also describes the privacy of their lifestyle and its 'considerable seclusion'. Shelley suggests that Victor is not interested in being popular: 'it was my temper to avoid a crowd' and prefers having one close friend in Clerval. Victor describes Clerval at length. He is a Romantic child, meaning he is imaginative, well-read and takes the lead in their childhood play. 'He tried to make us act plays' suggests that Victor perhaps was not as enthusiastic as Clerval but it is clear their relationship was strong. Victor describes it as the 'closest friendship'.

> **AO2** Brief reference to word use and meaning

> **AO3** Brief reference to context but undeveloped

> **AO2** Analyses language but focus drifts from question

This extract is about Victor's childhood reflections and he states that 'No human being could have passed a happier childhood'. He is aware of his early advantage in life but also I think sad given his present situation. He remembers his parents as embodying 'the very spirit of kindness' and how he was aware as a child that he was 'fortunate'.

> **AO1** This does not add very much to the argument

In the novel as a whole childhood is presented as a less happy state. Caroline, Elizabeth and Justine all experience difficult childhoods and are taken in by Alphonse, as wife, daughter and servant. Justine is treated as part of the family, despite her servant status. All are decent women despite their early hardship which shows that children exposed to kindness and care after deprivation can thrive later in life. This is more complicated in terms of the monster who can be likened to Victor's child. Shelley reveals through his story how an abandoned child seeks friends and protectors and that this process can be full of misunderstandings.

Paragraph 4

In summary, childhood is a key theme in the novel. Shelley presents the theme through Victor and the monster's perspective as well as detailing the childhood backgrounds of minor characters. She shows both how childhood should be a time of nurturing and what happens if a child is neglected or abandoned. Unlike his parents, Victor becomes a 'tyrant' who 'rules' the monster's 'lot' and pays the price.

Paragraph 5

Check the skills

Re-read paragraphs four and five of this response and:

- highlight other **points** made
- circle any reference to **context**
- underline any places where the student has made an **interpretation**.

Now you try!

Look again at paragraph three (*'This extract is about Victor's childhood reflections …'*) and improve it by:

- Changing the opening sentence
- Adding a comment about Victor's experience of being parented
- Ending with a **summary point** about the presentation of the importance of childhood and how this has been a **key idea** through the novel
- Improving the overall **style** by making sure your sentences **flow**; using **connectives** to **link** ideas

What does a Grade 7+ answer look like?

Read the task again, then the sample answer below.

4. Starting with this extract, how does Shelley present the importance of childhood in the novel? Write about:
   - how Shelley presents the theme of childhood in this extract
   - how Shelley presents the importance of the theme of childhood in the novel as a whole. **[30 marks]**

In the extract, Shelley presents childhood through Victor's nostalgic recollection as he tells his life story to Walton. A sense of lost innocence influences the narration as he looks back from his current despair. Pathos underlies his statement that 'No human being could have passed a happier childhood'. In the novel as a whole, childhood is associated with vulnerability and a need for nurture. Some characters, however, suffer deprived childhoods, with parents unable, or unwilling, to look after them, offering a poignant contrast.

Shelley reveals Victor's privileged childhood through language and tone. Pride can be detected in the formal expressions 'resided' and 'considerable seclusion' and social superiority in his indifference towards his 'schoolfellows'. This elitism is counterbalanced by warmth towards Clerval. Shelley suggests this relationship is cultivated by Victor: 'I united myself ...'. The intensity of Victor's childhood affection is expressed by the adverb 'fervently' and the superlative adjective 'closest'.

Victor's childhood influences are presented as positive. He implies that parents can make or break a childhood and that his were 'agents and creators', not 'tyrants'. Clerval's Romantic imagination directs their play and has a profound influence. Victor remembers his parents' 'spirit of kindness' and 'indulgence', later echoed in De Lacey. His awareness of a 'fortunate' upbringing suggests children understand more than adults think. This is mirrored in the monster's development, with his gradual awareness and ability to think independently, adding interest to the theme.

AO1 Clear opening statement focusing on theme

AO2 Apt quotation embedded with some language analysis

AO1 Structural link to presentation of theme in novel as a whole

AO1 Fluent introduction of new aspect to analyse

AO2 Well-chosen quotations; detailed language analysis

AO3 Good use of context linked to theme

AO2 Another skilful structural link with apt quotations

AO1 Strong summarising sentence

Another important aspect of the exploration of childhood lies in presenting Victor's as a time of creativity and freedom, with 'plays' and 'masquerades' as well as book learning. In this, Shelley is reflecting wider cultural debates of the time on what should constitute childhood and the degree to which parents should indulge their children. Victor's perception that 'gratitude' for his upbringing develops 'filial love' is echoed later when he fantasises about the relationship he will have with his creation: 'No father could claim the gratitude of his child so completely...' In reality, the monster has little to be grateful for.

Paragraph 4

Childhood is represented by Shelley in many ways. In the extract it is introduced via Victor's Romantic recollections and elsewhere it surfaces in the sad tales of Caroline, Elizabeth and Justine's childhood deprivations. It is portrayed in a complex way in the monster's narration of his early life. The monster's 'childhood' is the antithesis of Victor's. Shelley interweaves this theme to raise questions about responsibility, duty and nurturing and to draw attention to the dangers of both indulgence and neglect.

Paragraph 5

Check the skills

Re-read paragraphs four and five of this response and:

- identify any particularly **fluent** or **well-expressed** ideas
- find any further references to **context**
- highlight any places where the student has shown **deeper insight** and offered **original** or particularly **thoughtful** ideas or made interesting **links**.

Now you try!

Now, using the plan you made for Question 5 on page 75, write a full response. Here's a reminder of the question:

5. Starting with this extract, how does Shelley present the relationship between nature and nurture? Write about:

- how Shelley presents the relationship between nature and nurture in this extract
- how Shelley presents the relationship between nature and nurture in the novel as a whole. **[30 marks]**

- Try to match your answer to the High Level objectives on page 63.

Now you try!

Now, apply the skills you have learned to these two new questions:

- Note down key points from the extract.
- Select the key quotations you want to use from the extract.
- Repeat the process with other ideas from the novel as a whole.
- Write your answer.
- See **Answers** page 88 for a list of key points you could have made.

Read this extract from Chapter 15 about the monster's visit to old De Lacey.

> ' "By your language, stranger, I suppose you are my countryman; – are you French?"
> ' "No; but I was educated by a French family, and understand that language only. I am now going to claim the protection of some friends, whom I sincerely love, and of whose favour I have some hopes."
> 5 ' "Are they Germans?"
> ' "No, they are French. But let us change the subject. I am an unfortunate and deserted creature; I look around, and I have no relation or friend upon earth. These amiable people to whom I go have never seen me, and know little of me. I am full of fears; for if I fail there, I am an outcast in the world forever."
> 10 ' "Do not despair. To be friendless is indeed to be unfortunate; but the hearts of men, when unprejudiced by any obvious self-interest, are full of brotherly love and charity. Rely, therefore, on your hopes; and if these friends are good and amiable, do not despair."
> ' "They are kind – they are the most excellent creatures in the world; but,
> 15 unfortunately, they are prejudiced against me. I have good dispositions; my life has been hitherto harmless, and in some degree beneficial; but a fatal prejudice clouds their eyes, and where they ought to see a feeling and kind friend, they behold only a detestable monster."
> ' "That is indeed unfortunate; but if you are really blameless, cannot you
> 20 undeceive them?"
> ' "I am about to undertake that task."

6. Starting with this extract, how does Shelley present the theme of prejudice as important? Write about:

- how Shelley presents the theme of prejudice in this extract
- how Shelley presents prejudice as important in the novel as a whole.

[30 marks]

Read this extract from Letter IV in which Robert Walton writes to his sister, telling her about Victor. Then answer the question that follows.

> How can I see so noble a creature destroyed by misery, without feeling the most poignant grief? He is so gentle, yet so wise; his mind is so cultivated; and when he speaks, although his words are culled with the choicest art, yet they flow with rapidity and unparalleled eloquence.
>
> 5   He is now much recovered from his illness, and is continually on the deck, apparently watching for the sledge that preceded his own. Yet, although unhappy, he is not so utterly occupied by his own misery but that he interests himself deeply in the projects of others. He has frequently conversed with me on mine, which I have communicated to him without disguise. He entered
>
> 10 attentively into all my arguments in favour of my eventual success, and into every minute detail of the measures I had taken to secure it. I was easily led by the sympathy which he evinced to use the language of my heart; to give utterance to the burning ardour of my soul; and to say, with all the fervour that warmed me, how gladly I would sacrifice my fortune, my existence, my
>
> 15 every hope, to the furtherance of my enterprise. One man's life or death were but a small price to pay for the acquirement of the knowledge which I sought; for the dominion I should acquire and transmit over the elemental foes of our race. As I spoke, a dark gloom spread over my listener's countenance. At first I perceived that he tried to suppress his emotion; he placed his hands before
>
> 20 his eyes; and my voice quivered and failed me, as I beheld tears trickle fast from between his fingers – a groan burst from his heaving breast. I paused – at length he spoke, in broken accents: – 'Unhappy man! Do you share my madness? Have you drank also of the intoxicating draught? Hear me – let me reveal my tale, and you will dash the cup from your lips!'

7. Starting with this extract, how does Shelley present the relationship between Robert Walton and Victor Frankenstein?

Write about:

- How Shelley presents the relationship between Walton and Victor in this extract
- How Shelley presents their relationship in the novel as a whole.

[30 marks]

GLOSSARY

Literary or language term	Explanation
abstract noun	a noun that refers to feelings, concepts and states that do not exist physically (e.g. delight, hope, love)
antipathy	a feeling of dislike or hostility that a reader has for a character
apostrophe	the use of 'O' or 'Oh' to address a character who is absent or dead
antithesis	the direct opposite of something
bias	a strong feeling either for or against a thing; not based on fair judgement
archaic	a word or a phrase that is old-fashioned
cautionary tale	a traditional folk story with a moral message which serves to warn the listener
Chinese box	a frame narrative: where one narrative is inside another
climax	the high point of a play, act or story
dialogue	speech and conversation between characters
elegiac	a tone of sadness/lament for someone who is dead
emotive language	language used to move the reader to feel a particular emotion
epistolary	written form (a novel or story) as series of letters
exclamatory sentence	a sentence expressing strong feeling ending in an exclamation mark
Faustian imagery	imagery relating to intense suffering or an unnatural aspiration for knowledge and power, derived from Marlowe's play *Doctor Faustus*
first-person narrator	a teller of the story who refers to him/herself as 'I'
flashback	a scene or part of a play, novel or film that goes back in time, prior to the main story
foil	a character whose qualities contrast with that of another in order to highlight the other's traits
foreshadowing	a hint of what is to come in a work of poetry, fiction or drama
framed narration	a story constituting a frame for another story or stories
genre	a form of literature characterised by particular conventions of form, content and style
Gothic	in literature a genre that includes horror, the supernatural or eerie, romance and death
hyperbole	exaggeration to make a point or emphasise an idea
imagery	descriptive language that uses images to make actions, objects and characters more vivid in the reader's mind
leading question	a question that prompts or encourages the answer wanted
lyrical language	language that expresses emotion and feelings – often about the beauty of the natural world
metaphor	when one thing is used to describe another to create a striking image
monologue	an extended speech by one person

Literary or language term	Explanation
mood	the tone or atmosphere created by an artistic work
motif	a recurrent image or idea
narrative digression	a temporary interruption to the narrative
non-chronological	narrative that jumps forwards or backwards in time
pathetic fallacy	the natural world, often the weather conditions, reflects the emotions of a character
pathos	a quality in speech or writing that produces sadness or pity
personification	the treatment or description of an object or idea as though they were human, with human feelings and attributes
perspective	the point of view of a character
pronoun	a word that stands in place of a noun, e.g. 'her' instead of 'Elizabeth' or 'mine' instead of 'my tortures'.
realism	subject matter which feels true to life
repetition	repeated words or patterns
rhetorical question	asked for effect rather than for an answer
Romanticism	a style of literature during the late 18th and early 19th centuries that emphasised the imagination and the emotions
Russian doll	a frame narrative: where one narrative is inside another
science fiction	a type of literature in which the social impact of science, real or imagined, is explored
simile	when one thing is compared directly with another using 'like' or 'as'
sublime	a Gothic concept to describe grandeur of thought, emotion and spirit
superlatives	adjectives which indicate the most or greatest degree of a quality, e.g. 'biggest' or 'most beautiful'
symbolism	using something to represent something else, usually with meanings that are widely known (e.g. a dove as a symbol of peace)
term of address	the way in which a person is referred to, e.g. 'Victor', 'my dear Victor', 'Frankenstein'
theme	an idea running through a work of literature or art
tone	see mood
tragedy	a dramatic form in which the protagonist's fatal flaw results in his/her downfall
tragic hero	a protagonist whose flaws lead to his/her destruction and that of others
uncanny	strange and disturbing experiences and events in the Gothic genre
voice	all characters can have a voice, and the author has a voice, which can be a construct

ANSWERS

Note that the sample paragraphs given here provide only one possible approach to each task. Many other approaches would also be valid and appropriate.

PLOT AND STRUCTURE

Letters I–IV – Now you try! (page 7)
Walton's letters introduce the theme of friendship when Walton tells his sister that he needs someone 'who could sympathise' with him, 'whose eyes would reply' to his. The verb 'sympathise' and the image of responsive eyes suggest a deep, unspoken understanding. Walton has his crew for company but needs a friend like himself to confide in.

Chapters 1–4 – Now you try! (page 9)
The first four chapters introduce Victor's childhood interests and in particular his thirst for learning, when Victor refers to 'the secrets of heaven and earth.' This phrase is mysterious and biblical, with the abstract noun 'secrets' suggesting something hidden and 'heaven and earth' the idea of creation. The ambitious scale of Victor's learning is expressed with the extremes of high ('heaven') and low ('earth').

Chapters 5–8 – Now you try! (page 11)
The important theme of female goodness is explored in Chapter 8 when Elizabeth declares to Justine, 'I will melt the stony hearts of your enemies by my tears and prayers.' 'Tears and prayers' are gentle expressions of emotion by one virtuous woman on behalf of another. 'Enemies' and 'stony hearts' provide strong visual images of hostile jurors, with 'melt' suggesting a thaw, in response to female tenderness.

Chapters 9–12 – Now you try! (page 13)
The monster's natural curiosity about humans is explored in Chapter 12 when he refers to the De Laceys as 'lovely creatures'. The noun 'creatures' usually denotes animals rather than humans, and reminds the reader that the monster's understanding of the world is fuzzy. Nevertheless the fact that he 'longed to discover' 'motives and feelings' reveals an intense and developing need to understand.

Chapter 13–16 – Now you try! (page 15)
The significant theme of knowledge is explored in Chapter 13 when the monster says to Victor, 'Of what a strange nature is knowledge! It clings to the mind … like a lichen on the rock.' Shelley uses an exclamation 'Of (…)!' to express the monster's wonder. The following use of a simile 'like a lichen' reinforces the point, providing an image of knowledge as an organism, slowly attaching itself to its host.

Chapters 17–20 – Now you try! (page 17)
After the destruction of his mate, the monster's final threat foreshadows Elizabeth's death with, 'I shall be with you on your wedding night.' This implies a disruption to the celebration. Victor, however, misunderstands the target of the monster's threat, assuming he will be the victim. The monster's words build up the narrative tension and set up a dreadful scenario culminating in the shock of Elizabeth's murder.

Chapters 21–24 – Now you try! (page 19)
It is at this point in the narrative that Shelley shows Victor's loss of hope of leading a meaningful life when he thinks, 'but the apple was already eaten.' Shelley uses a symbolic reference to the fruit of the tree of knowledge in the Garden of Eden to reveal Victor's sense of inevitable tragedy. His actions, like the eating of the apple, cannot be reversed and the simplicity of his statement mirrors his bleak mood.

Walton, in continuation– Now you try! (page 21)
In the final letters Shelley contrasts Victor and Walton when she demonstrates Walton's sense of responsibility in his confession, 'If we are lost, my mad schemes are the cause.' With the ship ice-bound and the crew's lives endangered, Walton recognises his responsibility, reducing his lofty ambitions to 'mad schemes'. Victor, however, looking back at his life, doesn't admit his faults with similar honesty.

Form and structure – Now you try! (page 23)
Foreshadowing is an aspect of narrative form used throughout the novel to raise dramatic tension, for example in the monster's warning, 'And fear not but that when you are ready, I shall appear'. This anticipates not only a dramatic moment but also communicates his ability to observe without being seen. His language communicates power with its ironic use of the polite 'fear not' and the bold statement 'I shall appear'. This creates suspense for the reader.

Quick revision – Quick quiz (page 24)
1. As a warning. 2. Caroline is the daughter of Beaufort, his close friend, who falls on hard times. 3. Caroline finds Elizabeth living with a peasant family, and adopts her. 4. A merchant who wants Clerval to follow in his footsteps. Victor goes alone to Ingolstadt. 5. A 'syndic'. 6. Cornelius Agrippa (1486–1535), a German doctor and alchemist. 7. After nursing Elizabeth through scarlet fever. 8. Clerval. 9. The monster appears. 10. She let him wear the locket which she thinks provoked the murder. 11. Incriminated by the planted locket. Bullied into confession by a priest. 12. To help him recover after William's murder. 13. Monster appears and demands Victor listen. 14. Felix. 15. She is linked to their misfortune; suffers exclusion and prejudice. 16. Seeks friendship/acceptance. 17. She must be the same so he is accepted/loved. 18. He looks at the monster's face and loses trust. 19. 'I will be with you on your wedding night'. 20. Commit suicide.

Quick revision – Power paragraphs (page 25)
1. Shelley contrasts the beautiful and remote Arctic of Walton's imagination and its harsh reality.

Walton is excited when he writes: 'I shall satiate my ardent curiosity with the sight of a part of the world never before visited'. Later his anxiety is clear from the 'thick fog' and ice plains which 'close in' the ship. Shelley shows how the inhospitable and dangerous Arctic tests human resilience by exerting power over those who visit.

2. Shelley gives the impression of a very close relationship between the two. Walton affectionately refers to Margaret as 'dear' and 'excellent' and anticipates her concerns, reassuring her that he will 'do nothing rashly'. He also confides in her about his need for a close friend although he checks himself, 'Well, these are useless complaints' and tries to sound cheerful. He tells Margaret her letters 'support' his 'spirits' although we do not get to read any.

Quick revision - Exam practice (page 25)

• We learn that Walton sees himself as 'self-educated' and 'illiterate', not unable to read, but lacking a formal education. The image running 'wild on a common' suggests a free-spirited child but also, perhaps, a Romantic lack of cultivation. He was allowed to roam and have adventures and this is reflected in his favourite childhood reading 'books of voyages'. It can be assumed that these pastimes fed his imagination and led to the Arctic expedition.

• We learn that Walton sees himself as lonely with no-one to share feelings of possible success or failure. He confides that he needs 'the company of a man who could sympathise' with him, who understands his 'day dreams'. His Romantic imagination is suggested by 'sympathise' and 'day dreams'. He has a practical need for friendship and a need to talk to someone about his hope and ambitions.

SETTING AND CONTEXT

Science and revolution - Now you try! (page 27)

Shelley explores the context of revolution when the monster threatens Victor with 'Mine shall not be the submission of abject slavery. I will revenge my injuries'. His position of 'abject slavery' lacks dignity and he asserts his power to rise up and take 'revenge'. His defiant tone can be seen to reflect the industrial unrest of the time and the threat of 'mob violence'.

Romanticism and the Gothic - Now you try! (page 29)

Shelley presents Clerval as a Romantic figure when Victor, in Ingolstadt, reflects on Clerval's qualities and positive influence: 'Clerval (…) again taught me to love the aspect of nature, and the cheerful faces of children.' Clerval embodies the passions and ideals of Romanticism by his behaviour. His 'love' of 'nature' and appreciation of childhood innocence symbolised by 'cheerful faces' lifts Victor's spirits and temporarily empowers him.

Quick revision - Quick quiz (page 31)

1. Process of animating corpses through electrical charge. 2. The negative impact of new textile machinery on jobs/skills. 3. A British scientist who believed in science's power to create life. 4. 1789. 5. Being restored to life after drowning, fainting/nervous collapse.

'Apparent' and 'absolute' death. 6. The countryside around Ingolstadt; the De Lacey cottage in the forest; the lake in Geneva and the surrounding mountains; the Rhine Valley. 7. Victor's workshop in Ingolstadt; the hut in Orkney; the bed chamber in Evian. 8. a) Shelley married the Romantic poet, Percy Bysshe Shelley; she was with him and other Romantic writers in Switzerland when she started writing *Frankenstein*. b) Shelley had early experiences of loss and death. 9. Gloomy, enclosed and places of psychological/physical captivity. 10. Huge, remote and places of refuge or retreat.

Quick revision - Power paragraphs (page 31)

• Shelley describes the Arctic differently depending on character and perspective. For Walton it is a place of adventure and mystery. Initially it exists only in his imagination as 'a region of beauty and delight' with 'the wondrous power which attracts the needle'. His quest to get to the North Pole and find a safe 'passage' is his primary and practical motivation but he is clearly spurred on by his emotions and a desire to achieve.

• For the monster it is both a retreat and a setting where he is master. Walton appreciates the monster's 'rapid progress' by sledge. Later, in pursuit, Victor reads the message, 'Follow me; I seek the everlasting ices of the north, where you will feel the misery of cold and frost'. The monster withstands the climate and negotiates the terrain. For Victor the Arctic is a destination associated with toil and suffering, ending in death.

CHARACTERS

Victor Frankenstein - Now you try! (page 33)

Shelley shows how Victor is deluded in his ambition to create life by presenting his imagined thoughts of the future. He earnestly, but rather naively, states, 'A new species would bless me as its creator and source'. 'Creator' suggests that Victor sees himself as a god-like figure and 'bless' expresses ideas about the glory and honour he will enjoy. Shelley shows how Victor is getting carried away by pride and ambition.

The monster - Now you try! (page 35)

Shelley shows how the monster learns how to assert his power when he verbally threatens Victor with, 'If I cannot inspire love, I will cause fear.' The 'if clause' gives the condition of being unloved, while the main clause, 'I will ...' shows its result and is a loaded threat. The monster is determined to persuade Victor to create a mate for him and so Shelley adds this verbal power to imply he will use physical power if his needs are denied.

Robert Walton - Now you try! (page 37)

By the end of the novel, Walton reveals how his experiences have transformed his understanding of others when he describes his encounter with the monster. His feelings of awe are communicated in the statement, 'I approached this tremendous being.' The adjective 'tremendous' suggests Walton's respect and dread as well as the monster's size, and the abstract noun 'being' communicates his wonder at the monster.

Henry Clerval – Now you try! (page 39)

Clerval's positive effect on Victor is shown by Victor's praise and respect for him when he comments, 'Study … had rendered me unsocial but Clerval called forth the better feelings of my heart'. Clerval's therapeutic effect is clearly communicated by the phrase 'better feelings'. The 'heart,' representing the seat of the emotions, suggests that Clerval is as good for Victor's psychological health as he is for his physical health.

Elizabeth, Justine and the Frankensteins – Now you try! (page 41)

As Victor's younger brother, Shelley uses William to express the terror of meeting the monster with his cry, 'Monster! ugly wretch! you wish to eat me and tear me to pieces …' William's rejection is unbearably cruel from the monster's perspective but is understandable, given he is a child and very frightened. His behaviour triggers the monster's desire for revenge.

De Lacey, Felix, Agatha and Safie – Now you try! (page 43)

Shelley uses Safie to show how good can come from bad and how strength can come from adversity. The monster observes how 'the presence of Safie diffused happiness' in the De Lacey household. The abstract noun 'presence' has two meanings, physical and spiritual, and Safie's effect, as a welcomed cultural outsider, affects each family member in a positive way. Her character symbolises the power of love and its ability to overcome prejudice and oppression.

Quick revision – Quick quiz (page 44)

1. Happy. 2. He becomes obsessive about his studies. 3. Doubt and mistrust replace pity. 4. To kill the monster. 5. Communicate. 6. He discovers prejudice in an 'innocent' child, who turns out to be Victor's brother. 7. To maximise his revenge. 8. To take his own life. 9. An Arctic explorer writing to his sister. 10. Walton admires Victor and wants to befriend him. 11. To agree to turn back and to listen to the monster. 12. Loyal, supportive, puts Victor first. 13. His education and desire to travel to India. 14. Strangled – a revenge killing. 15. Kind, patient, strong and independent-spirited.16. Implicated by locket. Jury don't believe her. Makes a false confession. Victor doesn't tell the truth. 17. Alphonse, Caroline, Victor, Ernest, William, Elizabeth and Justine. 18. Doted upon, beautiful and the youngest. 19. Ideal father and protector, unprejudiced by appearances. 20. Brings happiness and love.

Quick revision – Power paragraphs (page 45)

1. Clerval can be viewed as Victor's foil because his personality, temperament and interests contrast with Victor's. He has a 'noble spirit', is level-headed and inspired by literature and these characteristics highlight Victor's emotional detachment, mood swings and obsession with science. Both have a passion for learning but Victor's is misdirected. Clerval puts Victor's needs before his own and ends up a sacrificial victim – the direct consequence of Victor's 'murderous machinations'.

2. Walton and Victor are ambitious men and both, to some degree, self-educated. Victor recognises the ambition in Walton when he says, 'Do you share my madness?' Although they both seek glory, Walton is the more sensible, who, in the end, puts the needs of his crew before his own ambition. Victor's attempt to intervene and persuade the crew to continue 'Oh! Be men (..)' reveals he has not learnt to rein in his passions.

Quick revision – Exam practice (page 45)

- Victor withdraws from his family because of excessive grief and guilt which cannot be fully expressed. On the lake he can gain 'peace' and enjoy nature's 'beautiful (…) heavenly qualities' that contrast with his own 'miserable reflections'. Victor's depression is profound but he is able to appreciate nature's ability to soothe a troubled mind. He seeks out this calm place to restore him although his state of mind is so low that he has suicidal thoughts.
- Victor considers suicide. He says he was 'often tempted to plunge into the silent lake' which expresses the frequency and strength of his suicidal thoughts. 'Plunge' suggests a spontaneous and energetic action and 'silent lake' a tranquil but very final welcome. Death is seen in two ways: as a means of escape of 'calamities' and a 'base desertion' of his duties to Elizabeth and Alphonse. The latter is what prevents him from taking his own life.

THEMES

Knowledge and ambition – Now you try! (page 47)

Shelley shows that some knowledge is difficult to accept when the monster expresses how learning can be confusing: 'Was man, indeed, at once so powerful, so virtuous and magnificent, yet so vicious and base?' Shelley explores the contradictions of human nature in this rhetorical question, using the adjectives 'virtuous' and 'vicious' – with opposite meanings but similar form – to emphasise the monster's confusion.

Nature versus nurture – Now you try! (page 49)

Shelley shows the monster is aware of the awful effects of a lack of nurture when he recollects with sadness, 'No father had watched my infant days, no mother had blessed me with smiles'. Shelley uses repetition, 'no father', 'no mother' to stress the negative consequences of abandonment and emotive language such as 'blessed' to create a poignant tone. The monster understands that his 'childhood' has been denied him.

Companionship and isolation – Now you try! (page 51)

The monster's understanding of the positive effects of companionship is revealed through his belief that his 'virtues will necessarily arise' when he lives 'in communion with an equal.' The words 'will necessarily arise' emphasise the certainty of his opinion and 'with an equal' spells out the conditions of his relationship with another, a similarity of status. His belief is based on his observations of the De Lacey household and his own negative experience of isolation.

Prejudice – Now you try! (page 53)

Shelley explores the way that prejudice is embedded in society in her description of the jury's verdict against

Justine: 'their settled conviction in the criminality of the saintly sufferer.' The phrase 'settled conviction' reveals how people hold firm to a view, regardless of whether others around them hold the same view. The use of 'criminality' with its negative meaning close to the alliterative and emotive phrase 'saintly sufferer' reinforces the error of their judgement.

Justice and revenge – Now you try! (page 55)
Shelley shows that justice is associated with effort and difficulty when the monster eventually goes to Victor to: 'seek that justice which I vainly attempted to gain from any other being'. The struggle is expressed in the adverb 'vainly', which conveys failure, and the verb 'seek', which involves the idea of an active quest. Shelley suggests that justice is not easily found, is hard to achieve and is often denied.

Quick revision – Quick quiz (page 56)
1. Ambition, discovery, knowledge, desire for glory, friendship, Romanticism, sympathy and compassion. 2. Victor, Clerval, the monster, the De Laceys, and, to a lesser extent, Walton and Alphonse. 3. Victor and Walton. 4. The 'serpent' is used in Victor's warning to Walton about the dangers of ambition; 'lichen' is used in the monster's description of the clinging nature of knowledge. 5. Victor. 6. Their love develops from nurture. 7. He is able to enter gruesome places to get body parts. 8. Clerval, the monster, the De Laceys and Elizabeth. 9. Good companions: Victor and Walton; Elizabeth and Clerval to Victor; the De Laceys to one another. 10. Physical and emotional, voluntary or enforced. 11. His female equivalent. 12. Grief, misery, frustration and obsession. 13. Clerval's father shows prejudice about education; Safie's parents suffer prejudice about race and culture/religion; monster suffers prejudice about his appearance; jury are prejudiced against Justine. 14. Thinks that William's youth means he is unprejudiced. 15. Monster goes to blind De Lacey, knowing he can't be prejudiced against his appearance; monster describes prejudice as a type of blindness as people can't see the truth. 16. He prefers the familiar to the unfamiliar face. 17. The monster. 18. Alphonse was a 'syndic'. 19. Justine's trial. 20. The monster on Victor.

Quick revision – Power paragraphs (page 57)
1. Shelley links the monster with nature from the beginning by showing his affinity with the natural world. His appreciation is reflected by the 'stream' which 'supplied' him with drink and the trees that 'shaded' him. He feels cared for by the natural environment. Later he goes to the Arctic, a hostile natural setting, but one which he has mastery over; like the mountains near Geneva, the ice plains of the Arctic are also a place of refuge for him.
2. Shelley uses a forest setting to locate the De Laceys to highlight their harmony with nature. Their rhythms are attuned to the seasons, with the monster observing how, as the 'sun became warmer', 'Felix was more employed'. The monster also learns that, despite being in 'perpetual exile' and living

in poverty, they are happy, particularly after Safie's arrival. The forest is free from the cultural prejudices of the city and allows them to live happily together.

Quick revision – Exam practice (page 57)
• Victor is shown to be at odds with nature. Shelley describes the extraordinary contexts of his work, 'the dissecting room and the slaughterhouse', causing his 'human nature' to 'turn with loathing'. Victor's intense disgust is shown by the noun 'loathing' and the implication is that what he sees is savage and inhumane. His work is isolating and, by necessity, is hidden and indoors. It makes him 'insensible to the charms of nature', meaning he has no direct relationship with nature.
• Victor's neglect of nature is reflected in neglect of family and friends as if they are one and the same. Summer is lyrically described as 'a most beautiful season' and 'never (…) a more plentiful harvest', with Shelley using a series of superlatives and comparatives for emphasis. Victor's inability to appreciate nature is explicitly linked to neglect of 'friends'. She suggests a harmonious link between an appreciation of nature and friendship, with Victor's 'silence' communicating something unnatural and worrying to Alphonse.

Imagery and vocabulary – Now you try! (page 59)
At the end, Shelley uses exclamatory sentences when the monster expresses intense feelings of grief about Victor, 'O Frankenstein! generous and self-devoted being!' These heighten the tone of his emotional distress. The use of the apostrophe 'O' is also moving as it signals Victor's death and the monster's feeling of immense sorrow.

Narrative style and techniques – Now you try! (page 61)
At the end of the novel, when Walton faces the crew's revolt, he questions himself with, 'Yet could I, in justice, or even in possibility, refuse this demand?' Shelley shows his mind at work, thinking through his options, wondering whether refusing the crew's request is firstly moral and secondly realistic. The fact that Shelley positions 'in justice' before 'in possibility' suggests that Walton's moral sense is dominant.

Planning your character response – Now you try! (page 67)
• **Paragraph 1**: Alphonse's tender love for William, 'lovely boy', 'anguish' at his death. Effort to control his emotions – concern for Elizabeth – tries to prevent her seeing corpse. Kind – doesn't exert power.
• **Paragraph 2**: He thinks of others before himself – Caroline and Elizabeth – is protective towards women. 'Her words pierce my heart.' Pleads with Victor. Importance of family and support.
• **Paragraph 3**: Victor criticises Alphonse's lack of guidance when he was young and reading – but otherwise his presentation is positive. He is always concerned about Victor's silence/withdrawn behaviour.
• **Paragraph 4**: Supports Victor when in prison.

Reminds Victor of his duties towards Elizabeth.
- **Paragraph 5**: Overjoyed at the prospect of the wedding – dies of sorrow. Poignant final image.

Grade 5 answer – Check the skills (page 69)
Points: Paragraph 4: Victor is pitied by others. He is cared for by Clerval and Elizabeth when ill. He abandons the monster and does not take responsibility. Paragraph 5: Walton admires and pities Victor.
Context: The power of nature is a Romantic idea and Clerval is a Romantic character.
Interpretation: Elizabeth's love for Victor also makes her pity him. Victor takes rather than gives pity/love. Walton's emotional response, when Victor dies, frames the novel and sways the reader's sympathy.

Grade 5 answer – Now you try! (page 69)
Victor's silence throughout the extract means that Shelley only describes his thoughts and feelings. When Shelley writes, 'But I the true murderer' it is *as if* Victor has confessed his guilt but he hasn't. The fact that he has these thoughts in the prison right by Justine's side but doesn't, or can't, confess is frustrating because Justine's life is in his hands. Victor's inability to take any action here or try to tell the truth is typical of his behaviour in the novel as a whole, where his secret compromises his actions. Victor is often silent and withdrawn. In Ingolstadt, for example, Clerval gently criticises Victor for not writing to his family and informs him they are 'uneasy' at his 'long silence'. In the prison cell he is physically close to Elizabeth and Justine but his silence is the result of despair. The reader at this point might feel pity for his distress or anger at his inability to act.

Grade 7+ answer – Check the skills (page 71)
Points: Paragraph 4: Victor's lack of compassion and failure to consider the effect of actions are character flaws. His friends and family are loyal but don't know the cause of his misery. Paragraph 5: Walton has the final say on whether Victor deserves pity. His pity for the monster, rather than Victor, closes the novel.
Context: Victor's ambition is 'Faustian'. Like the character of Dr Faustus, he sacrifices everything for his goals. Victor's decision not to tell Elizabeth his secret until after they are married reflects the patriarchal context in which they were living, when male power was not questioned.
Interpretation: Victor's inability to share his secret could inspire pity, but his decision to tell Elizabeth only when she is under his authority, could be seen as calculating. Walton's question anticipates his sister's confusion about his feelings towards Victor.

Grade 7+ answer – Now you try! (page 71)
AO1:
- In the extract, Shelley presents Alphonse's shock at William's death and a desire to protect Elizabeth.
- In the novel as a whole, Alphonse is a character who is nurturing and empathetic.
- Shelley makes Alphonse more active as the novel progresses.
- Towards the end, Alphonse asks Victor about his intentions towards Elizabeth.

AO2:
- Alphonse's references to 'my lovely boy' and 'my beloved William' show the depth of his loss.
- His pleas to Victor to return home and 'console' Elizabeth shows he understands their relationship.
- Alphonse looks forward to when Elizabeth and Victor are married and 'dear objects of care will be born'.
- Shelley leaves us with a poignant image of Alphonse as a weakened, vulnerable man 'sunk under the tidings' of Elizabeth's death.

AO3:
- The implicit criticism of Alphonse's carelessness as a parent, with regard to Victor's reading, suggests he should have done more to guide him. This links to the cultural debate of Shelley's time on the dangers of over-indulgent parenting.
- His desire to protect his family and the metaphor of his role as 'a good angel' 'enraptured' by Victor's acquittal draws on Romantic views of parenting.

Planning your theme response – Now you try! (page 75)
- **Paragraph 1**: Nature – 'environs of Ingolstadt' 'rambles of this nature' Clerval is the nurturer – the one who proposed the tour – link to similar examples in novel as a whole
- **Paragraph 2**: The power of nature 'salubrious' air and the power of nurture 'conversation of my friend'
- **Paragraph 3**: Clerval's efforts are always to care for, amuse and educate Victor; nature's power – De Laceys
- **Paragraph 4**: The monster's personal experience of nature and nurture – believes he was born good but society/lack of nurture made him evil.
- **Paragraph 5**: Different ways in which the thematic relationship is presented: nature and nurture in harmony (Clerval, the De Laceys, Elizabeth) or at odds (Victor, the monster).

Grade 5 answer – Check the skills (page 77)
Points: Paragraph 4: In the novel as a whole, childhood is presented as a difficult time with several female characters experiencing hardship. The monster suffers abandonment. Paragraph 5: Childhood is presented through the lives of major and minor characters.
Context: Shelley shows the consequences of abandonment and neglect and the importance of nurturing. There is some implicit knowledge of the contemporary debate about parenting and how children should be treated.
Interpretation: The female characters are all virtuous, despite having a difficult start in life. Disadvantaged childhood and later moral development are linked. Victor's parenting is tyrannical rather than benevolent and the monster later makes him pay for this.

Grade 5 answer – Now you try! (page 77)
Victor looks back at his childhood with some nostalgia, asserting that 'No human being could have passed a happier childhood.' This makes him sound not only aware of his early advantage in life but also, I think, sad given his present situation. He remembers his

parents as embodying 'the very spirit of kindness' and how he was aware as a child that he was 'fortunate'. Victor's parents gave him a stable upbringing and were child-centred in their outlook. Victor states they were not 'tyrants' but 'creators' of 'many delights' which makes them sound very loving. His childhood is presented as idyllic and contrasts with the way many characters' childhoods are presented in the novel.

Grade 7+ answer – Check the skills (page 79)

Points: Paragraph 4: Victor's childhood is creative and free. A child's filial gratitude is echoed when Victor considers the relationship he will have with his creation. There is a marked difference between Victor's fantasy and the reality of the monster's 'childhood'. Paragraph 5: Childhood is presented through Victor's personal recollection, the backstories of the female characters, and the monster's narration of his early life.

Context: Shelley reflects wider cultural debates of the time about childhood, parental responsibilities towards children and the negative effects of both neglect and indulgence. Victor's childhood includes Romantic ideas: the importance of creativity, freedom and the imagination to a child's development.

Interpretation: The monster's childhood is the very opposite of Victor's. The monster has little to be grateful for. The monster's 'poetic' presentation of the learning part of his childhood.

Grade 7+ answer – Now you try! (page 79)

AO1:
- Clerval's role as a nurturing presence is prominent.
- The power of nature, to restore physical and mental health, is made clear in this extract.
- In the novel as a whole Victor appreciates the power of nature as he embarks on journeys, some alone and some in Clerval's company.
- Shelley's presentation of nature/nurture makes the reader think about the dangers of ignoring them.

AO2:
- Clerval's role in drawing out Victor and teaching him again 'to love the aspect of nature' is nurturing.
- Victor is overwhelmed by nature's beauty when he describes 'a serene sky and verdant field'. This lyrical language suggests euphoric joy.
- The monster's early experience of nature's power is poignant as he 'gazes with wonder' and feels pleasure in 'the gentle light (…) over the heavens'.
- Victor's meddling with nature and rejection of the monster causes a disruption to the life he has created, to his own life and that of those he loves.

AO3:
- The beauty and awe-inspiring qualities of nature and its healing benefits reflects Romantic views on nature's therapeutic powers and the 'sublime'.
- The monster's experience of nature has a childlike wonder and innocence which typifies Romantic attitudes to childhood.

Practice questions – Question 6 (page 80)

AO1:
- Shelley presents the theme of prejudice in the extract through the dialogue between De Lacey and the monster.
- The extract shows how prejudice can be overcome when there is mutual understanding and a removal of barriers. It is the monster's appearance that causes the prejudice and De Lacey cannot see him.
- In the novel as a whole Shelley shows how prejudice is linked to fear and injustice and occurs for several reasons.
- Shelley reveals the devastating consequences of prejudice, and the power it exerts over humans.

AO2:
- De Lacey's friendliness and desire to show his awareness of a fellow 'countryman' shows how he is searching for similarities between them.
- The monster reveals his outcast status using adjectives with negative connotations: 'unfortunate' and 'deserted'.
- De Lacey's rational language 'in the hearts of men when unprejudiced…' contrasts with the monster's poetic language 'a fatal blindness…'
- The metaphor of blindness is a powerful one in the context of De Lacey's physical blindness.

AO3:
- Shelley was born into a family of radical thinkers interested in exploring social and political issues. This is reflected in the novel's presentation of prejudice.
- Prejudice as a theme is linked to oppression, fear, anger and injustice – all Gothic concerns.

Practice questions – Question 7 (page 81)

AO1:
- Shelley presents the relationship between Walton and Victor via the following devices in the extract: Walton's perspective as narrator; the mixture of emotions; the description of their actions; the one-sided dialogue.
- The attraction, admiration and respect Walton has for Victor is clear in the extract.
- In the novel as a whole there are parallels between the two. They identify with each other.
- Their similarities are clear from the beginning but at the end Walton accepts his responsibilities.

AO2:
- Walton's disclosure 'without disguise' and 'in minute detail' suggests openness and trust.
- Rhetorical question 'Do you share my madness?' is a recognition of Walton's ambition and its dangers.
- Victor's metaphorical language, 'the intoxicating draught' emphasises the intensity of his emotions.
- Walton's accusation, 'If you had listened … Frankenstein would yet have lived' shows his loyalty to Victor and a measured quality in his thinking.

AO3:
- Walton's language in the extract marks him out as a Romantic adventurer.
- The language of emotions, the metaphors in the extract and Victor's 'dark gloom' are Gothic features.